LITERARY DISTRACTIONS

LITERARY
DISTRACTIONS

by

R. A. KNOX

SHEED & WARD • NEW YORK

ACKNOWLEDGEMENTS

"R. L. Stevenson" (MS. ACC 2035) is here reproduced by courtesy of the National Library of Scotland; "G. K. Chesterton", by courtesy of *The Dublin Review;* "Pascal", by courtesy of the Philosophical Library, Inc.

CONTENTS

THE GREEKS AT SEA

THIS lecture is not really a lecture at all. It is an attempt to recapture, in my own mind, the nautical atmosphere of the Classics; to remember the great passages and the great periods concerned. I say, in my own mind; and that is a mind which, fifteen or twenty years ago, knew the Classics tolerably well; since then, the volume of its contents has shrunk to narrower limits; it is, after all, a very small stock-in-trade of information that the school-master needs in order to impress school-boys with a sense of erudition. And in the last few years this same mind has, alas, rusted altogether; only the occasional needs of a crossword have stirred up, now and again, the ancient memories; who am I, that I should lecture about the Classics? When the gradual realization was borne in upon me that I was committed to a Classical tour in the Mediterranean, conscience got to work. I understood from an undergraduate friend that when he travelled on one of these cruises he found the boat full of school-masters, who gathered in a little knot by the bulwarks every time land was sighted, and said to one another, "Est in conspectu Tenedos, notissima fama insula". The same, I began to anticipate, would be expected of me; and was I equal to it? Shame-facedly, I fell back on the school-master's refuge; I prepared the lesson. I would dig about among the Classical books which still collect the dust on my shelves, refurbish the mind with old tags, old gobbets of information; I would step aboard the *Argo*, not a Jason, indeed, but a Pelias revivified from Medea's cauldron. And, while I was about it, why be content with simply looking up the old references? Why not copy them

I

down, and string them together, and call the whole a lecture when I had finished it?

Let me banish at once any fears that may have been aroused by my title. I am, and have always been, a landlubber; this is the first time I have ever spent twelve continuous hours afloat. I do not intend, therefore, to crush you with technical information about ships, their rigging and their management; I know less about it, I suppose, than any soul here. No, what I would have liked to do would have been to reconstruct, for your benefit and for my own, some picture of what it was really like, going to sea in the old days; I do not mean fighting at Salamis, I mean simply travelling, say, as we are travelling, from Marseilles to Constantinople, in those days, Massilia to Byzantium. I mean, would one have had a cabin, and if so how large, and would it have had any natural light, and how would the sailors be dressed, and what kind of food would you get, and what kind of signals would you make, if any, when you passed another ship, and what sort of price would the tickets be, and all the thousand-and-one details that go to make up real life. It is an extraordinary thing about the Classics; here is a vast quantity of literature; learned people have read it all from end to end and digested it all in hand-books and Classical dictionaries and so on; and yet if you try to sit down and imagine what it would really have been like, to live through the ordinary actions of twenty-four hours in ancient Greece, or even in ancient Rome, you are constantly having your picture falsified by coming across things which the scholars don't know. It is no more possible to *imagine* the journey from Massilia to Byzantium in a Greek merchant ship than it is possible to imagine a day spent on the moon. So much for the antiquarians.

One or two obvious facts may, however, be laid down about the general conditions of sea-faring, which after all varied very little during the period we call the Classical period. Ovid, in the first century A.D., seems by his own account to have been exactly as uncomfortable on board ship as Odysseus a thousand years before him; and the Argonauts, if we may trust Apollonius Rhodius, did very much the same distance in a day as St. Paul did on his missionary journeys. You could cover 110 or 120 miles in a day and a night in a fast ship, a ship of war, and then only if you were pressed. When the Athenians decided on the destruction of Mitylene, and then repented of their decision, they sent out a second boat with tidings of the reprieve, which was to overtake the first boat, carrying orders for the city's destruction. The sea distance between Athens and Mitylene is 186 miles; and the first boat was a day and a night ahead of the second. The second boat, carefully prepared for the purpose by the Mitylenean ambassadors, set out to do a record time; they rowed and slept in shifts, and the rowers actually ate and rowed at the same time, which is, if we are to interpret the phrase literally, a very difficult thing to do. Paches, the Athenian admiral, had actually read the first decree and was about to put it into execution when the second ship reached the harbour with the reprieve. It is like one of those mathematical sums. Herodotus says that a ship can cover about seventy miles in a day and sixty in a night; perhaps their special rush arrangements allowed the second crew to do 140 in the twenty-four hours. On the morning, therefore, on which Mitylene was doomed to destruction the first boat was perhaps twenty-six miles away from its destination, going at eighty miles a day; the second was forty-six miles away, going at 140 miles a day, and the first reached port an hour or two before the second. That gives us some idea of the possibilities of ancient travel, when you were going at your leisure and when you were rowing against time.

The old warships seem to have used sail and oar indifferently, but to have preferred oars when speed was essential. The merchant ships carried both, but I imagine they only used their oars in case of emergency. About what you did with the oars when the boat was under sail, I can find no information and can form no picture. A merchant ship seems to have reckoned on doing an average of sixty miles a day; that is nearly always St. Paul's rate of travel, though a specially favourable wind could increase the pace considerably; in the last chapter of the Acts he did the two hundred miles between the Straits of Messina and Puteoli inside two days. But of course a merchant vessel would always be coasting if possible, and on principle would be likely, I suppose, to anchor for the night.

Those are the dull details. Now, what are the atmospheres of Classical sailing which I am trying to recover? Let us divide them, roughly, into periods. The first period is the Homeric, the fairy-story period, dating (or pretending to date) about a thousand years B.C., before the Greeks became a sea-faring people in any real sense. You get the key-note of that period in the famous question of the *Odyssey*: "O strangers, who are you, and whence sail you the watery ways? Is it on some business, or do you wander rashly, after the manner of pirates, across the sea, men that wander at the risk of their own lives, bringing harm to other folk?" It is obviously quite polite to assume that your guests may be pirates, and is indeed a sort of a compliment, because it assumes that they are not afraid of the sea, as any decent merchantman would be. If they were Phoenicians, it might be a different matter; but a respectable Greek would probably coast around from harbour to harbour, not taking any unnecessary risks. At no time did the Greeks love the sea; in the Homeric times they hated it. In the *Iliad*, of course, there is little opportunity for travel. But observe that in the first book, when the envoys are sent to give back the maiden Chryseis to her father, no less than eight lines are occupied with the description of their journey to Chryse, and nine lines to the description of their journey back. The whole distance is about thirty miles, along a perfectly unembarrassed coastline. Only an unfamiliarity with the idea of sea travel could make such a recital possible.

The *Odyssey* is of course a sea-epic from start to finish. But it would be a great mistake to represent it as a deliberate voyage of adventure. All Odysseus was trying to do was to navigate twelve ships from Troy back to Ithaca, off the west coast of Greece; and his wanderings were not self-chosen, but thrust upon him by contrary winds, by the displeasure of the gods, and so on. Odysseus is represented as crafty in a hundred ways; he knows how to make his escape when he is shut up in a giant's cave, or when an enchantress has turned his companions into swine; what he does not know is how to sail a ship—at least, there is no suggestion anywhere that he knows how to sail a ship. He knows how to *make* a ship; the manufacture of the raft on which he gets away from Calypso's island is a masterpiece of detail. But that only shews that the man who wrote the *Odyssey* understood how ships were constructed; it does not shew that he had ever sailed in one. And when you look into it I should say that the *Odyssey*, for a poem which is professedly about the sea all through, shews incredibly little knowledge of nautical actualities.

For one thing, I think you have the sense, in reading the *Odyssey*, that at the time when it was written a ship was a kind of new invention, of which people were still rather proud— at least in Asia Minor, if that is where the poem was written. Penelope is quite distracted with fear when she hears that her son Telemachus has crossed over from Ithaca to the mainland, a distance considerably shorter than a Channel crossing. "Why", she asks, "has my son gone? There was no need for him, surely, to mount up on ships, which are to men the horses of the sea, and so they cross over much wet." This, mark you, is supposed to be a queen born and bred on an island; an island where it was notoriously impossible to ride on horseback, because there was no level country; yet she talks about ships as "the horses of the sea". And, just as a teetotaller will always talk about beer as "liquor", so this landlubberly queen will describe the sea as "wetness"; it is something quite strange to her. And when Odysseus at the end of the story has to expiate the slaying of the suitors, he is to carry an oar on his shoulders and go with it inland until he comes to a people who ask him why he is carrying a winnowing-fan on his shoulder, people who have never heard of ships or of the sea. That is just the kind of conceit which would occur to a story-maker to whom the whole idea of sea travel had still something of strangeness and novelty. Oh, I know they tell us there were sailing vessels in the Aegean before 2000 B.C., but even if the scholars are right, I feel they must have been rarities. The *Odyssey* is very particular about describing all the minutest details of navigation, putting up the mast and hoisting sail and casting anchors and so on, re-peating the formula on every possible occasion. The ship was a new toy, something like what the aeroplane is to us.

If the writer knew something about ships, he certainly knew very little about the Mediterranean. It is quite evident from the first that the *Odyssey* is meant to deal with strange, un-explored worlds in which you may meet any kind of monster or strange people, "the Anthropophagi, and men whose heads do grow between their shoulders"; it is a sailor's yarn, a tall story, which is only likely to go uncontradicted if it confines its descriptions to parts of the world which its audience has never been to. If Homer had been a Viking, writing for Vikings, it would have been probable enough that he should have assigned these strange adventures with sea-monsters and one-eyed giants and the old man who kept the winds in a bag to the Mediterranean. Living in the Mediterranean as he did, why did he not transfer them to the Black Sea (where the Argonauts went), or to the undiscovered coasts that lay beyond the Straits of Gibraltar? Clearly because in his day the Mediterranean itself, or rather the western part of it, was a world sufficiently undiscovered. Homer knows the Ægean; knows the coast of Egypt, and the winds that drive you down to it if you are not careful how you round the southernmost point of Greece. But the Sicilians are a mere name, only once alluded to; and they are barbarians evidently, not Greeks. Surely it is clear that he is writing at a time when it is safe, if you like, to say that Sardinia was full of magic cows, or that the souls of the dead resided somewhere on the west coast of Italy, because nobody is in a position to correct you.

I know M. Bérard went all round the Mediterranean in a yacht, and wrote a book of two thousand pages in which he tried to identify accurately all the chief points at which Odysseus touched. But you can do anything when you resort to such methods of identification. If Homer meant the *Odyssey* to be the record of an actual cruise, why are all his indications of distance and direction so vague? "So on we sailed, sad at heart, glad to escape death, but lacking our dear companions"—that is the way in which Odysseus keeps his log. Contrast it with the orderly navigation of Virgil's *Aeneid,* and you find yourself in a different world at once.

There are pictures from Homer that I should have liked to see on this cruise. I should have liked to see the coast of Ithaca; "a rugged land, but a good nurse of heroes, nor can I ever see a sweeter sight than my own country". I was asleep, I am sorry to say, when we found the coast on which Hector cast fire among the ships of the Greeks. But I did not hope to hear the Sirens, or catch sight of the smoke rising from Circe's roof, because I know they were never really meant to be there; they were just people in a story.

That is the legendary period of Greece, when the sea is a strange thing and an enemy. Then follows the heroic age of Greek navigation. Upon my word, the history of those 250 years, 750–500 B.C., reads more like a fairy-story than the *Odyssey* itself. It was the age of Greek expansion. During that time, a handful of mainland, Asiatic or island states had planted the whole of Sicily with colonists, and had dotted Greek stations all along the Sea of Marmora, both sides of it, and along the west and north sides of the Black Sea. In all, thirty cities had sprung into being in the western part of the Mediterranean, the westernmost being our port of embarkation, Marseilles. And during the same period, twenty-four cities had sprung into being in the Sea of Marmora and the Black Sea, the furthest of them being right up in the Crimea. How on earth did they do it? Of those fifty-four colonies, five were founded by Megara alone. Megara was a town with a very small territory attached to it, which had the advantage of being situated exactly on the Isthmus of Corinth, so that it commanded the sea in two directions. But what can have been the size of it? Athens, the largest city of ancient Greece, possibly numbered two hundred thousand free citizens in the whole of its territory of Attica; but this was at the time of its greatest development, just before the Peloponnesian War. That is to say, it had about the same population as Plymouth. Megara was only a tenth of the size of Attica, and I doubt if its population can ever have exceeded twenty thousand, which is about the population of Bexhill. Yet of these five colonies three became far more important than the mother city itself; and one of them, Byzantium, the goal of our journey, has been one of the world's great cities ever since. Miletus, on the Asiatic coast, was more energetic than Megara itself; it produced twelve separate foundations in the same period. These ridiculous little sea-side resorts would send off some fourth of their total numbers to a distant and barbarous territory—it might be nine hundred miles away, or nine days' fast travel; and there they would dig themselves in with a stockade and elect magistrates and all the rest of it, and grow into great walled cities, exporting corn to Greece as fast as they could grow it. The enterprise of the medieval Italian towns, or of Elizabethan England, pales by comparison with it.

Did the Greeks, in these days of their expansion, turn into splendid old sea-dogs, never happy unless they were reefing tight under a strong sou'wester, or whatever the phrase is? There is no evidence of the fact. I wonder whether the literary pose of great devotion to the sea is really a genuine one? We value such sentiments as a patriotic heritage, we English.

A wet sheet and a flowing sea, a wind that follows fast,
And fills the white and rustling sail, and bends the gallant
    mast;
And bends the gallant mast, my boys, while like the eagle
    free
Away the good ship flies, and leaves old England on the lee.
O for a soft and gentle wind! I heard a fair one cry;
But give to me the snoring breeze and white waves heaving
    high;
And white waves heaving high, my lads, the good ship tight
    and free—
The world of waters is our home, and merry men are we.

The author of that song was Allan Cunningham, a native of Dumfriesshire, who lived by journalism in London and, from all I can read of his biography, never ever saw a more agitated piece of water than the Solway Firth. Now let us turn to Alcaeus, a poet who flourished just at the end of this glorious age of colonization, an islander, too, from Lesbos.

"I cannot understand" (he writes) "the discordant state of the winds; for one wave rolls from this side, and another from that side; and we are carried about in the middle of it all with the black ship."

Thus Alcaeus; from the point of view of conscious heroism he is not much advanced on Hesiod, two hundred years earlier, who frankly admitted that he had spent all his life in Boeotia, except once when he went across to Euboea, which is about the same distance as from Hampshire to the Isle of Wight. No, love of the sea does not reflect itself, even now, in Greek literature; and I fancy these migrations were dictated more by sheer necessity—the need for getting rid of surplus population—than by any desire of adventure for its own sake.

Yet this age of adventure has left its mark on Greek literature. Its spirit still breathes in the record of Herodotus, though at the time of which he wrote the force of the movement was already spent. You may read there, how Xerxes when he came to the Hellespont and bridged it, found the Greek ships still passing through, with their cargoes of corn from Russia bound for the Greek mainland—like cheeky school-boys, one fancies, pretending not to notice that they are observed by the eye of a hostile authority. And there is that splendid scene at the Ionian congress, when Cyrus had already reduced the Greeks of the Asiatic coast to subjection, and the islanders were for surrendering themselves too; it was then that Bias of Priene, one of the seven wise men of Greece, proposed a wholesale emigration of all the Ionian colonists to Sardinia, where they could make a fresh start without threats of Persian interference. And indeed there was one city which refused slavery. The citizens of Phocaea were among the most adventurous of the Greeks; they had sailed as far as Tartessus, and made a treaty of alliance with a Spanish chieftain there. Leaving their city to the Persians, they sank a lump of lead in the harbour, and took a common vow never to return there until the lump of lead rose to the surface; and so they set out over the high seas in search of a new home. They went to Chios, and offered to buy the islands of Oenussae from them; the Chians refused. So they went back to Phocaea, massacred the Persian garrison, and set sail for the west. They landed in Corsica, and set up their temples there; for occupation, they raided their barbarian neighbours, until the Etruscans and Carthaginians sent out a punitive expedition. There was a sea-battle, in which the Phoceans were victorious, but lost most of their ships; and, thinking Corsica too hot to hold them, removed to the southern coast of Italy, where at last they made a permanent foundation, the city of Velia. Remember that these men travelled with their wives and children, and the images of their gods; it was the migration of a people.

The spirit of such enterprises has been caught up unexpectedly by the poet of another tongue. When you read the third book of Virgil's *Aeneid*, you must not be tempted to think of the Trojans as merely cruising about in a dozen small ships, like the companions of Odysseus. It was the whole remaining population of Troy that took ship with Aeneas: "They came from all sides," we are told, "prepared alike with courage and with provision for the journey, ready to go into any land whither I might lead them." They, like the Phoceans, had their false starts; in Thrace, in Crete, in Carthage; at last, like the Phoceans, they settled in Italy, but with more glorious auspices, for the city they founded there was the direct ancestor of Rome. And I think that in recalling the spirit of those earlier days Virgil was almost consciously escaping from the present; from the over-civilized, jaded atmosphere of the early empire. Horace, at least, sought that inspiration; he has described, in words which have become hackneyed, the speech of Teucer when exiled by his father from Salamis:

> Where fortune bear us, than my sire more kind,
>   There let us go, my own, my gallant crew.
> 'Tis Teucer leads, 'tis Teucer breathes the wind;
>   No more despair, Apollo's word is true.

Another Salamis in kindlier air
  Shall yet arise. Hearts, that have borne with me
  Worse buffets, drown to-day in wine your care;
  Tomorrow we recross the wide, wide sea.

And elsewhere, recalling the example of the Phoceans, he has called on his fellow-countrymen to leave behind them the shores of Italy, drenched in all the blood of the Civil Wars, and sail out into the Atlantic to found a new home in the mythical lands of the sunset:

  What better counsel in our sad debate
  Than the grim oath of that Phocean state?
  Their fields they left, their homes and temples bare,
  For boars and ravening wolves a welcome lair.
  Whither the main-sheet tugs across the foam,
  The sport of East and Southern gales we'll roam;
  For us, the sundering ocean of the West,
  Its happy fields, and islands of the blest,
  Where, year by year, the untilled harvests shine,
  And, without pruning, burgeons still the vine.

There is something in the atmosphere of those early sea-adventures that touches the imagination of the poet in the stifled air of cities. And in our own unhappier age there are few appeals that strike the mind with a cleaner sense of re-generation—Scott Holland pointed it out many years back—than Yeats' early poem, "I will arise, and go now, and go to Innisfree". "The sea", says Euripides' Iphigenia, "washes away all evil among mankind."

But I am wandering from my theme. After the age of sea-adventure comes the age of the great sea-battles, beginning with the defeat of the Persians at Salamis in 480, and ending with the capture of the Athenian fleet by the Spartans at Aegospotami in 405. That period, so full of glory and of

tragedy, is fully documented not only in the literature of
Greece but in the literature of the world, and needs, therefore, the less recalling to memory. Salamis, with the Greek
fleet of little more than three hundred sail facing the enormous
navies of Persia, catches one's breath in anticipation of the
issue as I think no other battle does, whether you follow it in
the detailed narration of Herodotus or in the vaguer poetical
form which it assumes in the *Persae* of Aeschylus. "And anon,
at the word of command, they smote the surging brine with
the plash of their foaming oars, and all became swiftly plain
to the enemy's sight. First in good array the right wing led
in order, and then the whole fleet followed out; and as it
went you might hear a great cry, O sons of the Greeks, go
forth; set free your country, set free your children and wives,
and the temples of your fathers' gods, and the tombs of those
that went before; for all these now you go to do battle." After
Salamis the easy victories, the harassing of the Persian retreat,
the re-establishment of Greek influence on the Aegean sea-
board. Then the confederacy of the whole Greek race, with
its treasury at Delos; then the fatal influence of Athens, turning
a confederacy of free states into an empire dependent on one
naval power; those Attic ships, that once had vindicated the
freedom of the world, now coasting round from harbour to
harbour, dunning the sulky tributaries for their arrears of pay.
And so the greatness of Athens rises on the ruins of Greek
freedom, till at last the wrongs of little Megara force the hand
of the Spartans, and Greece splits into two camps, for the
great war whose history is the epic of Thucydides.

I think you can say that there is a sea-breeze blowing through
every page of Thucydides' history. By preference, I suspect he
was a landsman; he does not seem as fond of his occasional
nautical technicality as Xenophon, or as St. Luke. But from
the first you are conscious that this is a contest which will
have to be decided by sea-power; and when, at the end of the

truce, the Athenians refuse to give back the ships which have conditionally surrendered themselves after the blockade at Pylos, you feel, angrily, that they have won the war by a trick. But we are still only at the beginning; the climax of the war is only reached when Athens sends out her expedition to Sicily, by way of overawing the Greeks there into joining her alliance. No armament, we are told, so magnificent and costly had ever been sent out by any single Hellenic power; and the description of its setting out is worthy of the occasion. "Early in the morning of the day appointed for their departure, the Athenian forces and such of their allies as had already joined them went down to the Piraeus and began to man the ships. . . . The citizens came to take farewell, one of an acquaintance, another of a kinsman, another of a son, and as they passed along were full of hope and full of tears; hope of conquering Sicily, tears because they doubted whether they would ever see their friends again. . . . When the ships were manned, and everything required for the voyage had been placed on board, silence was proclaimed by the sound of the trumpet, and all with one voice before setting sail offered up the customary prayers; these were recited, not in each ship separately, but by a single herald, the whole fleet accompanying him. On every deck both the officers and the troops, mingling wine in bowls, made libations from vessels of gold and silver. The multitude of citizens and other well-wishers who were looking on from the land joined in the prayer. The crews raised the paean and, when the libations were completed, put out to sea."

So it passes out of our sight, the ships racing as far as Aegina, and turns at last westwards, the greatest expedition ever sent out from Athens. Through all its early successes, the shadow of its final defeat hangs over it, until that last great battle in the harbour of Syracuse, when the Athenian army, lining the cliffs, saw its fleet routed by the Syracusans and their allies, and knew that all hope of return to Greece was cut off.

"The last chance of the Athenians lay in their ships, and their anxiety was dreadful. The fortune of the battle varied, and it was not possible that the spectators on the shore should all receive the same impression of it. Being quite close and having different points of view, they would some of them see their own ships victorious; their courage would then revive, and they would earnestly call upon the gods not to take from them their hope of deliverance. But others, who saw their ships worsted, cried and shrieked aloud, and were by the sight alone more utterly unnerved than the defeated combatants themselves. Others again, who had fixed their gaze on some part of the struggle which was undecided, were in a state of excitement still more terrible; they kept swaying their bodies to and fro in an agony of hope and fear as the stubborn conflict went on and on; for at every instant they were all but saved or all but lost. At length the Syracusans and their allies put the Athenians to flight. . . ." The army was left to die in a hopeless battle, or to meet with life-long slavery in the stone-quarries of the island. So ended the Sicilian expedition.

The war still lasted another nine years; and the rally of the Athenians after a quite unparalleled disaster is one of the most remarkable achievements in history. The operations have now taken on a curious character. The war is almost exclusively a naval war, and the seat of it is almost exclusively Ionian; it is confined to the Asiatic coast and the Sea of Marmora. What had happened was that the loyalty of the maritime cities to the short-lived "empire" of Athens had been rudely shaken by the Sicilian disaster; most of them were ripe for revolt, and meanwhile the Spartans had been learning by experience, and were beginning to understand the importance of challenging the Athenians on the unfamiliar element. Accordingly, Peloponnesian fleets sail up and down inciting the subject-allies of

Athens to revolt; Athenian fleets sail up and down the same waters suppressing revolt where it has occurred, strengthening loyalty where it remains, and, above all, calling in the overdue arrears of tribute. There are comparatively few naval engagements; the fleets seem to avoid one another where it is possible. On the whole, you may think of it as an inglorious series of smash-and-grab raids; yet there are heroic moments. Conon is one of the great Athenian admirals; and there is something of the seventeenth-century sea-dog touch about his opponent Callicratidas, who boasts that he will stop him "making a mistress of the sea". And throughout the story you find a human relief in the strange career of Alcibiades, attaching himself now to one party of combatants, now to the other, yet always finding people to trust him.

In the middle of this period, Thucydides' history comes to an end, and Xenophon takes up the tale. Xenophon has a simplicity of phrase which sometimes makes his effects almost more telling than those of Thucydides. Listen to his description of the astonishing return of Alcibiades from an exile during which he had thrown in his lot recklessly with the enemies of his country. "He did not disembark at once, for fear of his private enemies; but standing on the deck he looked round for his friends, to make sure that they were present. Then he saw Euryptolemus son of Pisianax, his cousin, and others of his friends and partisans with him; and so he disembarked and went up to the city, with a crowd of followers prepared to protect him against all molestation. . . . He was put in autocratic control in all departments of state, as the one man who could preserve the old predominance of the city." But his triumph is short-lived; he is once more disgraced, and goes off in a private capacity to the Dardanelles. There, on the northern shore, the Athenian fleet is anchored, with the Spartan Lysander watching their movements from further along the coast; he does not come out to attack them, and the Athenians think he is afraid. Alcibiades pays a visit to the Athenian generals, and points out to them that they are making a mistake by keeping their camp in the open, instead of having their base at a walled city. They tell him to mind his own business; he is only a private citizen now. They continue in their ill-omened encampment, at Aegospotami, from which they have to go off every day by land to Sestos, to get provisions. "But Lysander, when this had been going on for four days, told his followers, when they saw the Athenians disembark and disperse themselves about the peninsula . . . to sail back to him, and signal to him by lifting up a shield in the middle of their voyage. They did as they were commanded. And Lysander immediately signalled to his ships to set sail with all speed; and Thorax followed with the land army. Conon (one of the Athenian generals), seeing the attack, signalled to the ships to rally in full force. But the crews were scattered ashore; some of the ships had only two-thirds of their complement, some one-third, some were altogether unmanned. So Conon and the seven vessels with him, together with the ship *Paralus*, put out to sea; all the rest Lysander captured off the shore." That is Xenophon's unemotional description of the amazing surprise action which at last brought Athens to her knees.

Curiously, after this the naval arm loses most of its interest for the historian of Greek warfare. The great battles of the fourth century are land battles; the empire of Macedon rose to power as a land empire. And the period of the great Athenian orators, Demosthenes and the rest, brings with it a fourth period of my lecture—you will be glad to hear that it is the last. We meet for the first time, in the private speeches of Demosthenes, a quite fresh sea-atmosphere—that of the ordinary merchant captain going out on a private cruise to the Black Sea or elsewhere, with a cargo for sale or exchange. It is a somewhat inglorious record, for it is a record of the law-courts, and what actually occupies our attention is, naturally enough, the criminal aspect of the matter. We learn all the dodges by which fraudulent men of business managed, even in those early times, to outwit their creditors and the underwriters. Here is Phormio, who sails for the Bosphorus, after raising twenty *minae* from Chrysippus on the security of his cargo. When he reaches port, he finds his goods are unsaleable, and he has no cargo to put on board for his return journey. So he sends word that he will ship his return cargo on a later boat; then waits till he hears that a boat bound for Athens from the Bosphorus has gone down with most of her crew, whereupon he pretends, and brings witnesses to prove, that this was the boat on which his imaginary cargo had been embarked. Here is Artemon, who on returning to Athens does not bring his ship into port, but conceals her in a bay only used by smugglers and pirates, and then represents her as having gone down in the Black Sea, so that he is not liable to repay the money lent him on the security of the cargo of wine which she carried. Here are Hegestratus and Zenothemis, natives of Marseilles, who overinsure their cargo and then are found by the passengers deliberately trying to scuttle the ship in mid-ocean. Here is Dionysiodorus, who is under contract to bring back a cargo of corn from Egypt to Athens, but, hearing that the price of corn has fallen in the home market, sells his corn in Rhodes, under the pretence that his ship is disabled, and never goes back home to meet his creditors at all. They are not edifying stories, but they serve to remind us of the background to all this business of colonization and of naval warfare—the economic necessity of importing goods, especially corn, into Greece proper. And they serve to give us some picture, even if it *is* a disedifying one, of real life among the Greeks. But, as I say, I do not think it is really possible to form any notion of what Greek sea-travel was like, for the ordinary passenger. The fact is, I suppose, that the Greeks didn't like it, and not liking it, left us no account of it, except an occasional allusion to its discomforts. There is Lucian, of course, but Lucian is decidedly A.D.

Another effect of their not liking it is, that you very seldom come across any description of scenery by a Greek author, in which the sea (as seen from the land) figures prominently. There is, of course, the unforgettable *pontion te kumaton anerithmon gelasma* of Aeschylus, "the myriad laughter of the sea's waves". But on the whole the sea is to the Greeks a treacherous element, dark, misty, interminable, fishy, tempestuous— anything except beautiful to look at, until you reach Theocritus and the Alexandrian period. It is in Theocritus that you will find Galatea sporting amid the sunlit waves; it is in Theocritus that a shepherd can wish he could sit with his shepherdess in his arms, "looking at our flocks as they graze together, and out over the Sicilian sea".

I have tried, with this collection of familiar incidents, to repeople the coasts through which we are travelling with some echoes, some ghosts, of their former inhabitants. I know that I have failed, but I feel that the failure is inevitable; something has come between us and the old Classics which makes their world, try as we will, a dead world to us. In illustration of that idea, may I call up one more famous sea-memory from an author of the first century A.D.—I mean, that mysterious passage in Plutarch's essay on the dying-out of the Oracles? Epitherses, the father of Aemilianus the orator, "said that once in sailing to Italy he embarked on a ship which carried a cargo and a large number of passengers. When it was already evening, near the Echinades islands, the wind sank, and the ship on its course came near Paxae. Most of the company were awake, and many were still drinking their wine after dinner. Suddenly a voice was heard from the island of Paxae, crying out, to their astonishment, for Thamus. This Thamus was an Egyptian pilot, unknown by name to most people on board.

Twice he kept silence when called, but the third time he answered whoever it was that called him. And this other, raising his voice, said: 'When you are at the Palodes, tell them that the great Pan is dead . . .' Thamus decided, if there was a wind, to sail past taking no notice, but if there was a windless calm at the place in question, to give the message he had heard. When they came opposite the Palodes, there was neither wind nor wave; so Thamus, looking out from the stern towards the land, said, as he had been told: 'The great Pan is dead.' No sooner had his voice died away than there came a great groan, not of one voice but of many. The company being numerous, the story quickly got about Rome, and Thamus was sent for by the Emperor Tiberius." The Emperor Tiberius—it is not strange that Christian authors should have been prepared to date the incidents more accurately. The great Pan is dead, and the world of which he is the symbol; we can never recapture it. And I knew that when I saw the Hellespont. It did not remind me of the ship *Argo,* nor of the agony of Troy, nor of Xerxes' bridge, nor of the Spartan victory at Aegospotami. The last, to me, is as legendary as the first. It was peopled for me instead by those who fought and died there fifteen years ago, men of my own country and of my own speech.

GOING ON PILGRIMAGE

WHEN the Holy Year comes round, we are all a good deal worked up about pilgrimages. Those of us who are going out to Rome are wondering about how long their money will last, and what the accommodation will really be like when they get there and whether it is possible to talk to Italians in French. Those of us who aren't going have—let us confess it—a slightly uneasy conscience about the thing. Is it very idle of us not to go? Is it rather unadventurous of us not to go? Is it a bit presumptuous to think that we can get on without the indulgences which we should gain if we did go? Doesn't it look as if our faith must be a bit weak, that we shouldn't want to go? In a word, oughtn't we to go?

So I thought I would talk to you this evening about pilgrimages. Not about the Roman pilgrimage in particular, because I dare say many of you have heard all you want to hear about that, but about pilgrimages generally; the idea of them and the history of them and so on. I don't know anything about them which any of you couldn't have found out for himself or herself by digging about in encyclopaedias; but somehow it looked as if it was me that had got to do the work—it generally is—and you will have to be content with what I've managed to dig up for you. But do let us start straight away by getting rid of that word "ought". When you ask if you ought to do a thing, you mean, Are you bound to do it? Bound in conscience? And of course you are not bound in conscience to go to Rome, any more than you are bound in conscience to go to Lourdes or anywhere else. Going on pilgrimage isn't something you are bound to do, like going to Mass on Sundays; it's an extra, like doing the Stations. And the whole point of those extras, of course, is that they aren't things you're made to do but things you would like to do for the love of God. I say "like to do", because it's a misleading habit of ours to imagine that the only way to please God is to do something you dislike very much. But that isn't true; the way to please God is to love him so much that you do what you think he wants you to do, at this and every moment, whether you like it or not. And there are plenty of other ways in which we can shew our love for God besides going on pilgrimage. If you have made a vow to go to Rome, and no obstacles have cropped up in the meantime which make it difficult for you, then you are bound to go to Rome. If your confessor had imposed a penance on you (as they sometimes did in the Middle Ages) of making the Roman pilgrimage, then you would be bound to go to Rome. As it is, it's something that's left to your choice.

If you were a Mahommedan, it would be different. Mahomet laid it down to his followers that each of them had a duty of going to Mecca at least once in his lifetime. So you see, going on pilgrimage isn't entirely a Christian idea. Why should it be? As long as there are particular places in the world which are capable of stirring your imagination because such and such an event happened there, because such and such a person is buried there, you will always find people wanting to visit such places. After all, if an aeroplane crashed in the next village, you would want to go and see the wreck of it; you don't quite know why, it's just ordinary human curiosity. In the same way, if you are travelling about the country, you will go a mile out of your way to see the site of some old battle-field, the ruins of some old castle; why not? You are a man, and the doings of your fellow men interest you, though it was all so long ago. Now, the instinct of pilgrimage is, I

take it, this same human instinct of ours, only (as the psycho-
logists would say) "sublimated". Curiosity is there, if you go
to see the Church of the Holy Sepulchre at Jerusalem, or the
Carmel of Lisieux. But this instinct of curiosity is overlaid
with something new; with feelings of awe and of devotion; you
must take off the shoes from your feet—you are standing on
holy ground. Some influence, you feel, must reach you, even
after all these years, from the hallowed spot which is so bound
up with the history of your religion. A pilgrim is a sightseer
endowed, if I may put it in that way, with a kind of second sight.

Christians of the first age, before the breach between
Church and Synagogue was complete, evidently went up on
pilgrimage to the Temple at Jerusalem according to the old
Jewish tradition. St. Paul, though he was regarded as the
apostle of the Gentiles, was making such a visit, and in fulfil-
ment of a vow, at the time of his arrest and imprisonment.
It is likely enough that this habit persisted until the destruction
of Jerusalem by the Roman armies in A.D. 70. When the
Romans rebuilt the city, sixty years later, they were at pains
(it would seem) to cover up all the sites which were regarded
as holy, whether by Jews or by Christians, and the Jerusalem
pilgrimage must have been a dull affair. But the Cenacle was
still shewn—the one holy place which afterwards became inaccessible to Christians, because the Mahommedans built a
mosque there, identifying it as the tomb of David. (I wonder,
was it? If so, it is interesting to imagine St. Peter on the day
of Pentecost standing just outside the Cenacle and reminding
his fellow countrymen what it was. "I can say this to you
about the patriarch David without fear of contradiction, that
he did die, and was buried, and his tomb is among us to this
day." You can imagine him slapping the wall as he said it.
But all that is very uncertain.) From A.D. 200 onwards, if not
earlier, Christian people were visiting the Cenacle, and also
(it would appear) the cave at Bethlehem.

At the same time, even in those very early days, people had started coming to Rome as pilgrims, and from as far away as Persia. They came to venerate the tombs of the Apostles, and more than once, if the legends are to be trusted, were surprised at their devotions and turned from pilgrims into martyrs themselves. But Rome, in those days, was so much the centre of the world that a great many people had business there at one time or another, and the habit of worshipping at the tombs of the Apostles would become common without any organized stream of pilgrims to account for it. Nor, while the empire remained heathen and Christians were always liable to persecution, was it probable that they should go in crowds to any shrine, however celebrated. It was not till the Empress Helena went out to the Holy Land in about 330, by which time her son Constantine had turned the Roman Empire Christian, that the rage for pilgrimage began. By the end of that century St. Jerome will describe to you streams of pilgrims making for the Holy Land, and churches had already been built on some of the most venerable sites, in Jerusalem and elsewhere.

There's a curious difference, I think, between the idea of pilgrimage as it existed in those days and the idea of pilgrimage you and I have. We think, say, of Lourdes as a place which is an uncomfortably long way off, and our notion is simply to get there, get there as quickly as possible and come back as quickly as possible when we have finished saying our prayers. But the Christians of the early centuries behaved as if they wanted to spin out their pilgrimages as much as they could. After all, in those days the civilized world was all grouped round the Mediterranean in a most convenient way; there were very few Christians in Britain and St. Patrick hadn't started in on Ireland. The Mediterranean isn't much more than two thousand miles long, and sea-travel wasn't frightfully slow—St. Paul covered sixty miles in the day when he wasn't being shipwrecked. So a pilgrim even from Spain, if he took the shortest way, would be at Jerusalem in little over a month. But that wasn't the way they did things; they went overland, and took their time over it. The earliest pilgrim who has left us an account of his travels—that was in 333, when the Empire had only just turned Christian—started at Bordeaux and went through northern Italy and the Balkans, along the Danube to Constantinople, and then across Asia Minor and Syria. He came back by a different route, but the only bit of sea-travel he put in was across the Adriatic from Durazzo to Brindisi, which is no distance. Of course, sea-travel was no doubt pretty uncomfortable, and he may have avoided it for that reason. But I think there was a deeper motive. Half a century later a Spanish nun went on pilgrimage and spent three whole years wandering about the Near East. Why did they want to make such a long job of it?

I think you can say that, although they visited holy places wherever they went, these people travelled for the sake of travelling. I don't mean that they found it comfortable, went abroad to see the world as you and I might. Nor do I mean that they found it uncomfortable, and did it for that reason, in penance for their sins; that idea became fashionable rather later, in the Middle Ages. I think they just wanted to get away from the world, from the people and the scenes they knew, in order to get closer to God. It was the same period, you see, which produced the Fathers of the Desert, and their idea, too, was to get away from the world, to be free from its entanglements, and alone with God. A hermit, living out in the desert, or a wanderer, never sleeping to-night in the same place as last night—it was all the same thing. Some people, having started out for the Holy Land, never came back. St. Jerome settled down at Bethlehem, and spent his time, to the great annoyance of his contemporaries, in making a new translation of the Bible. Before long, a holy widow, Laeta,

25

came and settled down near him with her daughter; they too wanted to get away from the fashionable world and say their prayers. The most extraordinary story of pilgrimage is that of St. Alexius, who is said to have left home on the night of his wedding, spent seventeen years as a pilgrim in the East, and then returned to Rome, where he spent the remaining seventeen years of his life disguised as a beggar in his own father's house. His collect, which we say every year, asks that we may learn to follow his example, which is perhaps going rather far. But I'm afraid it's not quite certain how much of it is true, the story of St. Alexius.

In the seventh century the Moslems conquered Palestine, and stayed there; those were lean times for pilgrims. But pilgrimages went on, and it was largely the ill-treatment of Christian pilgrims by the Mahommedans which led to the First Crusade. It was soon after the Norman Conquest that a Christian army took Jerusalem and set up there a Latin kingdom which lasted for nearly two centuries. Naturally Christian people were more eager than ever to visit the Holy Places, and all through the Middle Ages it seems to have been common form to go out there, even if you didn't fight in the Crusades. You might do it out of piety, or, as I said just now, you might have it given you as a penance for some very grave sin. The word "palmer" which you come across sometimes in books of Sir Walter Scott's, for instance, meant a pilgrim who had been out to Jerusalem and been given a badge of palm to attest the fact of his visit. In the East, where the distances aren't so great, this habit of visiting the Holy Land has never died out, either among the Catholics or among the schismatics; and the Crimean War, which only happened a hundred years ago, was largely caused by the fact that Russia (a curious thought) wanted to be the champion of Christianity in the Near East and take back the Holy Places from the Turks. But somehow, in Western Europe, the thing seems to have died out since the Reformation. How many people have you met who have been out to Palestine as pilgrims? How many pilgrimages (not pleasure-cruises, but pilgrimages) to Palestine have you seen advertised? The odd thing is that I shouldn't be surprised if the present Israeli Government, which is rather keen on encouraging the tourist traffic, succeeds by sheer advertising in making Christians from the West revive this forgotten medieval habit.

However, we must go back to the Middle Ages. All this time, the Roman pilgrimage was booming; Rome was so obviously the centre of the religious world, was such a treasure-house of relics, that there could be no doubt of that. The institution of the Holy Year can't be proved to go back beyond the Middle Ages themselves. The first such occasion of which we have any record is the jubilee year proclaimed by Boniface VIII in 1300. But, curiously, it is on record that what persuaded him to do it was the representation made by certain aged pilgrims that the same thing had happened a century before. By 1200, then, or perhaps even earlier, it had become customary to attach special indulgences to the Roman pilgrimage every hundred years. This was contrary to the spirit of the old Jewish law, which kept a jubilee every fifty years, and in 1350 the Holy Year was proclaimed again. The numbers taking part in these celebrations were extraordinary; it was calculated that in 1300 the population of the city was, on any given day, 200,000 above normal; and Dante compares the souls in hell to pilgrims passing over the Ponte Vecchio, which (coming from Dante) is a high tribute to the popularity of the jubilee.

Meanwhile, other centres of pilgrimage were beginning to take high rank. The most noticeable of these was the pilgrimage to Compostella, in Spain, where the body of St. James, son of Zebedee, was believed to rest. As we know, he was martyred by King Herod at Jerusalem, and even if it is true that he was the Apostle of Spain, we should not expect him to have left his relics there; they were said to have been miraculously transported to Spain at the time of his death. But, even so, all record of the fact seems to have perished at the time, and it was not till A.D. 800 that the relics were identified, through a vision granted to a Spanish monk. Nor did Spain enjoy an undisputed title; they claim to have the body of St. James at Toulouse (as the French sacristan said, in shewing off the head of the local patron saint, "Malheureuse-ment, il y en a deux"). But whatever the truth about the relics, or the way in which they came to Compostella, the shrine enjoyed enormous popularity, perhaps because Spain, during the Middle Ages, stood for a symbol of the conflict between Christendom and the infidel Moors. To this day, if you take a vow to go to Compostella, nobody under the Holy Father himself can release you from it.

I don't think the medieval pilgrim worried much about the historical evidence for this or that relic being genuine; he was probably more influenced by statistics of miracles, just as a lot of us are to-day. Next after Compostella, he would probably have recommended you to go to Loreto; and Loreto again is a bit of a head-ache for the historians. The story is that in the year 1291 the Holy House in which our Lady and St. Joseph lived at Nazareth was miraculously transported to Illyria (that is Jugo-Slavia) and thence to Italy. But it seems clear that there was a well-known church at Loreto dedicated to our Lady before the year 1291, and we have no evidence that a Holy House of this kind was ever pointed out at Nazareth itself. Nor is it clear that the story of the transportation was known at the time; the first undisputed documents on the subject date from 180 years afterwards. But there is no doubt it was a favourite place of pilgrimage, and its popularity survived the Reformation; the French mystic Malaval, alluding to pilgrimages in a book published in 1669, says "To

Compostella, for example, or Loreto", obviously mentioning the two first instances that occurred to him.

As I say, I think there was a certain difference between the earlier and the later notion of pilgrimage. At first, you thought of it as a way of detaching yourself from the world; St. Peter had told us that we ought to regard ourselves as strangers and pilgrims on earth, and certain pious people wanted to do that literally. Later, during the Dark Ages, the consciousness of sin weighed more heavily on men's minds, and pilgrimage became a form of penance. Nowadays we are so accustomed to the idea of rushing about the world seeing sights that we think of going abroad as a treat; but in earlier times travel was very uncomfortable and rather dangerous, and anybody who wanted to have a good time stayed at home. The fact that a place like Compostella or Loreto—still more, the Holy Land—was a long way away made it all the more desirable as a pilgrimage centre, because it let you in for a larger amount of mortification. But there was another motive, after all, for pilgrimage; it was a common thing, when you were in desperate need, to take a vow that you would go on a pilgrimage if your prayer was granted. And not everybody could afford the time to go wandering across Europe, so it was more practical to confine yourself to pilgrimage-centres nearer home. That meant that in every country there were shrines which you were encouraged to visit; places where our Blessed Lady was said to have appeared, or where the body of some well-known saint was preserved. Loreto was all very well for Italians, but surely the divine mercies were at work outside Italy.

So, Walsingham grew famous, and the shrine of St. Edward at Westminster, and above all the Canterbury pilgrimage to St. Thomas à Becket which has left such a mark on our literature. In Scotland, you had Dunfermline and St. Andrews. But there were lesser pilgrimages springing up all the time. In the

Middle Ages, the canonization of saints hadn't been tightened up as it is to-day, and if you had a devotion to the memory of some king or bishop or other great man you started making pilgrimages to his tomb, without waiting for the Church to tell you whether he was really a saint or not. Some of us will remember from our history-books the name of Simon de Montfort, the great Earl of Leicester, who gave us our first Parliament. His body was kept at Evesham, where he fell in battle, and there was a record in the abbey of about 130 miracles which were attributed to his intercession—yet, as far as I know, there was never any talk of canonizing him. More important still was the devotion to Henry of Windsor, that is, King Henry VI, who almost certainly would have been canonized if King Henry VIII hadn't quarrelled with the Church at the wrong moment. We have the account of some 175 miracles for which he was responsible, and these were extracted from a list which contained about 450, preserved at Windsor. By the end of the fifteenth century, it looked as if the Windsor pilgrimage were going to rival the Canterbury pilgrimage in popularity. Whenever anything went wrong with you, but more especially if it were some accident that looked as if it must prove fatal, your first thought, whatever part of the country you came from, was to ask for the intercession of King Henry and to promise, if all went well, a pilgrimage and a little offering at Windsor. Somewhere in St. George's Chapel you would find a shrine blazing with huge tapers, some of them more than a man's height, with crutches hanging on its walls as they hang in the grotto at Lourdes, with wax tablets representing the strangest scenes and the most undignified situations. There is record of the Windsor pilgrimage surviving right up to the time of the Reformation, so that the last of the pilgrims were jeered at, as they went on their way, by the Protestant inhabitants of the town.

That was, I suppose, the normal kind of pilgrimage at the

end of the Middle Ages, a pilgrimage undertaken to express thanksgiving for favours received. Chaucer, in the introduction to his Canterbury Tales, seems to take that as a matter of course; people go to Canterbury to visit the blessed martyr who has helped them when they were sick. And I suppose that was one reason why pilgrimages began to be looked on as a bit of a tea-party. If you hadn't got to go overseas, the journey after all might not be too bad; there was plenty to eat and drink at the Tabard. And you weren't necessarily feeling, at the moment, particularly pious. You had felt pious enough when you found your little son had fallen into a mill-stream, and you had to invoke some saint or other to get him out. But it wasn't necessary to fulfil your vow immediately; weeks had gone by, and perhaps months, and the immediate sense of relief had lost its vividness. You had to keep your vow and go to the shrine, but you weren't feeling extra pious on the journey, or even when you got there. Chaucer's pilgrims are a mixed lot, and some of them told stories which don't seem very edifying. They rather enjoyed their journey, it would seem, and perhaps the other people at the Tabard Inn looked over their shoulders at them a bit and said, "Huh! Pilgrims!"

But there were worse scandals than that. It was all very well to send a man on pilgrimage when he had committed a murder, as a good heavy penance; but if there was a lot of that sort of thing it didn't necessarily produce a very good type of pilgrim, the sort of person you would want to meet on a dark night. And then, this habit of roving about from one shrine to another probably attracted a certain number of rolling stones who would turn tramps nowadays, idle people, deserters from the army, people who had got into trouble. When you had got a good many of them, with their pilgrim's staves, collected in one place it was apt to breed something of a cup-tie spirit; if quarrels arose, there would be heads broken. And so, in one way or another, by the end of the Middle Ages the thing had got a bad name. The *Imitation of Christ* tells us that people who go often on pilgrimages are seldom the better for it, and there were critics, like Erasmus, who said much harsher things about it than that. Even before the Reformation, people were beginning to wonder whether the whole idea of pilgrimage wasn't being overdone. And the Holy Year of 1500, just before the Reformation, is said to have drawn fewer pilgrims to Rome than any Holy Year before or since.

The Reformation came, and in the reformed countries the idea of pilgrimage died out. Or rather, perhaps we ought to say that the practice of pilgrimage died out, not the idea; for after all the greatest literary achievement of Protestant England is the Pilgrim's Progress. But, of course, Bunyan did not hit upon the notion of pilgrimage as a symbol of spiritual adventure for himself. I wonder, had he ever come across the "Parable of a Pilgrim" that was written by the Carthusian, Walter Hilton, in his book *The Ladder of Perfection*? It is a singularly beautiful piece of English, and might have helped to form Bunyan's style, as well as giving him material. "I am nothing, I have nothing," says that earlier pilgrim, "and I desire nothing in this world; and I care for nothing but the love of Jesus, that I may see him in peace at Jerusalem." That old idea, from whatever source, Bunyan took over, and the England of his day had enough race-memory left to thrill with the romance of pilgrimage. But the practice had died out, here as in the other Reformation countries, except where a few furtive Catholics made their way to Holywell, in the wildest part of Wales; St. Winifred, they say, has never been without her clients for the last thousand years.

Even in those countries which remained true to the Faith there was a different atmosphere. The Holy Year, to be sure, was a more flourishing institution than ever in the days of the Counter-Reformation; the challenge thrown down by Luther had rallied the sympathies of Catholics more than ever to the Holy See. But the little local pilgrimages do not figure much in Catholic literature between 1500 and 1800. Piety took other forms; Jesuits and Capuchins were rushing about trying to rally the faithful with retreats and missions and catechisms; the old, leisurely ways were forgotten. The Enlightenment of the eighteenth century was not fond of childish things. Yet, curiously, it was that century which produced the best-known pilgrim saint of Christendom, Benedict Joseph Labre. After trying vainly to enter the novitiates of the Carthusian and Cistercian orders, he decided to spend his time in wandering from shrine to shrine, never seeing or writing to his family. For seven years he went on tramp, quite penniless, sleeping on the ground; from Loreto to Assisi, from Assisi to Compostella, from Compostella to Einsiedeln, he was always on the march. Then for six years he lived as a beggar in Rome, and died of exhaustion on April 16, 1783; this next Sunday is his feast.

What is it that has driven us back, during these last hundred years, to pilgrimage? Partly, no doubt, it is antiquarianism; we have rediscovered the Middle Ages, and the Gothic, and we set our faces towards Walsingham in deliberate imitation of our medieval forefathers. Partly, again, it may be due to ease of communication; supply does create demand, and when somebody flies out to Rome, as somebody did the other day, in time for luncheon and comes back the same afternoon, it makes you feel a little lazy doing nothing about the Holy Year. But there must be something more to it than that; Ars and Lisieux, Lourdes and Fatima—there seems to be a revived instinct among Christians for going and seeing the place for ourselves. Perhaps Divine Providence is making us more internationally-minded, by forcing us to rub shoulders with foreigners who are our fellow Catholics; in these days, heaven knows, we need it. Perhaps it is a rebuke to our modern intellectualism that we should find ourselves thus sent to school (as it were) with very simple people like St. Bernadette and St. Theresa for our school-mistresses. I am not concerned to discuss the inwardness of all that. I only want to register my impression that, for whatever reason, pilgrimage has a strong appeal for most Catholics in our own day—not a cultivated, not an antiquarian, but a genuine, spontaneous appeal. And it is worth while to consider, by way of winding up a rambling paper like this, how the modern spirit of pilgrimage differs from, how it resembles, the spirit of pilgrimage that was common among our forefathers.

I think there is a quite obvious difference; when we go on pilgrimage, it is a kind of corporate act; each of us goes as one of a crowd, and means to be one of a crowd; he wants to lose himself in a great popular demonstration—he is not just thinking about his own soul and his own needs. No doubt, if you consult the history of any great shrine, you will find the record there of people flocking in there centuries ago, one after another, past all counting. And naturally pilgrims did go in groups, as soon as the Roman Empire became Christian; it was safest, in days when there were robbers about, to travel in convoy. But that was only for convenience; each pilgrim was a lonely unit to start with. You can see that in Chaucer's Canterbury Tales; the company which sits down at the Tabard is a company "of sundry folk, by adventure fallen in fellowship"; they did not come from the same diocese or from the same parish. Nowadays the normal thing is to take part in an advertised pilgrimage, surrounded by your neighbours. The reason for that is obvious; everything is mass-produced nowadays, and the cheapest way to go to Lourdes is to go in a crowded train at reduced fares. But the effect of that is to alter, a little, the spirit in which we go. You are not concerned to get away from the world you know, like those old pilgrims of St. Jerome's day; on the contrary, if anything the world is too much with you. Nor are you concerned, like the pilgrims of the Middle Ages, to do penance for your sins; if you want to think about your sins you go into retreat, or attend a mission. Rather, you want to do penance for the sins of the world in general, to do penance for them, as far as that is possible, corporately; it is such public penance that our Lady enjoined at Lourdes, enjoined at Fatima. "We are all in the same boat"—that is the thought which rises in our minds as we swarm up the gangway at Dover; all in the same boat, members of the same human race, conscious of a common load of guilt.

But at the same time we do, like our forefathers, believe in the existence of holy places. Not only at Bethlehem or at Nazareth, but wherever God may appoint, sometimes the partition between this world and the next seems to wear thin, and the supernatural shines through; God keeps tryst with man. We are not so sure of our facts, perhaps, as people were in old days; is it certain that the body of St. James rests at Compostella? Is it certain that the children at La Salette saw what they thought they had seen? We may have to be content, here and there, with probabilities, even with possibilities. But we do believe that there are scenes in the world so charged with the influence of the Christian devotion which has surrounded them for centuries, that you cannot approach them without a thrill of veneration; and that in such scenes God does offer no ordinary graces, to the soul which approaches them humbly, and expectantly, and in a spirit of faith.

ON ENGLISH TRANSLATION

ACCORDING to a recent paragraph in the newspapers, translators who are members of the Institute of Linguists have decided to increase their charges. The present rate for translating French, German, Italian, and Spanish into English is £1 18s. a thousand words, and the proposed new rate will be two guineas; and so on through the gamut of the languages until you reach the translation of English into Arabic, which will now cost £8 15s. This institute is, I take it, the trade union of those useful people who compose for us the directions on medicine-bottles and the regulations at air-ports. Their highest skill is called into play when they act as interpreters at international conferences, for which they propose to charge anything between ten and sixteen guineas a day. All honour to them; but alas, their knell is sounded; a few years now, and they will be redundant. A process which they would be the first to describe as "automation" will have provided us with electronic typewriters which translate as they go along, and head-phones through which we can listen, at first hand, to the political grievances of the world. Parthians, and Medes, and Elamites, and dwellers in Libya about Cyrene, we shall hear them speak in our tongues the wonderful works of Man.

These are the artisans, the demiurges, the manufacturers of equivalents. They correspond, let us say, to the jobbing carpenter who runs up, and varnishes, a couple of book-shelves in that niche in the dining-room. At the other end of the scale are the artists, the Grinling Gibbonses of translation, exquisite workmen in detail; a scholar here, a poet there, who

36

thinks it is time he produced the absolutely perfect rendering of *Persicos odi*, or of *Animula vagula, blandula*. He works neither for fame nor for reward; he has simply taken a bet with himself, as it were, that the thing can be done, and cannot sleep sound till he has done it. Between these two extremes lies the craftsman. Of such was Chippendale; nor is the race extinct—one died in Yorkshire the other day, and left the business to his sons. In translation as in carpentry the craftsman is concerned to produce something useful but not merely functional; it is to represent the original in a graceful, a genuine, a solid form; the rendering, like the original, is to be a literary production. It is of him, the craftsman, that I would speak. How far is it possible to achieve this ideal, and what rules should govern the process?

Mr. Savory in his recent book, *The Art of Translation*,[1] has given us a list of twelve propositions, arranged in the form of thesis and antithesis, which will help us to decide this question. I think, on closer analysis, you can reduce the issues to two:

(i) Should a translation be literal first, and literary afterwards? Or the other way round?

(ii) Has the translator done his job, if he expresses the sense of his original in any style or idiom he chooses to employ? Or is he bound, in some way, to represent the style and idiom of his original?

Of course if you are translating for the benefit of the student, who wants to hold the text in one hand and your rendering in the other, literal you needs must be. But in so far as you succeed, you have produced a crib. A translation is meant for the reader who, having no skill or perhaps no opportunity to consult the original, expects to read you with the same interest and enjoyment which a reading of the original would have afforded him. On that subject, surely, the last

[1] Jonathan Cape, 1957.

word was said by the business man who declared that he could read Jowett's Plato "with his feet on the fender".

It will be seen that I am taking sides in the controversy. Books are meant to be read, and the first quality of a book is that people shall read it and want to go on reading it. You have done a disservice to your original if the reader puts your translation down almost at once, saying to himself, "I expect this stuff would be rather fine, *if one knew Greek*." You have got to make him say "This *is* fine", whatever sacrifice of literalness it may involve. I know well enough what stone will be cast up at me; I shall be told that the Authorized Version is an absolutely literal rendering, which is at the same time a fount of pure Jacobean English. It is, no doubt, painstakingly literal; though it does not quite come up to the standard of that American commentator who will give you, in the 80th Psalm, the rendering, "Jahweh Sabaoth, why dost thou smoke during the prayer of thy people?"[1] But is it, in the strict sense, good English? The statement, often rashly made, that our greatest writers have modelled their style on it, has been devastatingly refuted by Professor C. S. Lewis. He points out that although English literature is encrusted with quotations and half-quotations from the Bible, English style has been quite unaffected by the Authorized Version—you have only got to read a paragraph of Bunyan to be convinced of it. And if it has not been a model for authors, why should it be a model for translators? The truth is that Bible English is a language of its own; a hieratic language, deeply embedded in the English mind and perhaps indispensable to the ordinary Englishman's religion; but not a model to be imitated, because its idiom is foreign to us.

I say a foreign idiom, not in the sense that it is unintelligible, but in the sense that it is artificial. We know what is meant by "the God of Abraham and the God of Isaac and the God

[1] Briggs on Psalm 80 (79), verse 5.

of Jacob", but it is a Hebrew twist; if an Englishman speaks of the train to Bletchley and the train to Rugby and the train to Crewe, he means three separate trains, not one. And so it is all through the sacred text, from the first chapter of Genesis, where we read "God saw the light, that it was good" down to the last chapter of the Apocalypse, where the phrase "Without are dogs and sorcerers" has to carry the meaning "Dogs and sorcerers are not allowed inside". I do not say that you will be held up often, perhaps not more than five or six times in any given chapter, by these Hebraisms or Hellenisms, but you would not tolerate them anywhere else. Matthew Arnold actually gives us,[1] as an instance of "good, straightforward English", St. Peter's protest to our Lord, "Be it far from thee, Lord; this shall not be unto thee." But what Englishman ever said or wrote, "This shall not be to you"? It is not even Greek; what peeps out at you is the ghost of an underlying Aramaic.

Upon my word, the only piece of translation I know which is modelled on the Authorized Version is Milton's rendering of the *Ode to Pyrrha*. This also I have heard recommended as a model to beginners. But what a model!

> Oh, how oft shall he
> On faith and changéd gods complain, and seas
> Rough with black winds and storms
> Unwonted shall admire,
> Who now enjoys thee credulous, all gold;
> Who always vacant, always amiable,
> Hopes thee, of flattering gales
> Unmindful!

That is not English. Since our language has no terminations by which we can distinguish between nominative and accusative, masculine and feminine, only an inference from the context

[1] *On Translating Homer*, p. 90.

can determine which was credulous and which was all-gold, Pyrrha or the young man. Complain, if you will, that Sir Edward Marsh strays too far from the Latin when he renders *Cui flavam religas comam, simplex munditiis?* by "wrought upon thy lovely head that easy miracle of curling gold". But he has tried to catch some echo of Horace's magic, and of Horace's scorn. Milton's "Plain in thy neatness" he rightly stigmatizes as "word for word, but not grace for grace".[1]

It may, of course, be suggested that whereas the Authorized Version does not serve as a perfect model for English syntax, it is the standard by which we can best judge English vocabulary. This claim is actually made by Arnold in his lectures on translating Homer; "the translator", he says,[2] "cannot do better than take for a mechanical guide Cruden's Concordance". He has just given us a specimen of how he would like to see Homer turned into English hexameters. He has appealed to Cruden, to Cruden he shall go. He has used the following words which are not to be found in the Authorized Version: coward, skulk, let (in the sense of "allow"), future, warlike, foeman, transport, loom, pail (instead of "bucket"), redouble, and mounded. In two dozen lines he has given us eleven words for which there is no warrant in Scripture. And that is not in the least surprising; the vocabulary of the Authorized Version is extraordinarily limited. There are thirty-eight separate Hebrew verbs which are all represented, in the Old Testament, by the one verb, "to destroy". In the great literary efflorescence of the Elizabethan age, the revisers of 1611 were at pains to reduce, not to extend, the scope of Scriptural vocabulary.

I have called them revisers, and it is important to remember that they are properly so described. Very few English people realize how old, in its essential features, the English Bible is. Look at this passage from Coverdale:

---

[1] *The Odes of Horace,* i, 5. [2] *On Translating Homer,* p. 100.

Though I spake with the tongues of men and angels, and yet had not love, I were even as sounding brass, or a tinkling cymbal. And though I could prophesy, and had all faith, so that I could move mountains out of their places, and yet had not love, I were nothing. And though I bestowed all my goods to feed the poor, and though I gave my body even that I burned, and yet had not love, it profiteth me nothing. Love is patient and courteous, love envieth not, love doth not frowardly; is not puffed up, dealeth not dishonestly; seeketh not her own, is not provoked unto anger, thinketh no evil; rejoiceth not over iniquity, but rejoiceth in the truth; beareth all things, believeth all things, hopeth all things, suffereth all things.[1]

One is struck by the differences: the word "love" has been cut out, to be replaced in the Revised Version, and "courteous", with its pleasant Chaucerian associations, has gone. But what I wish to insist on is the resemblance. The translation of 1611 is not a document of Jacobean English; essentially, it dates from nearly a hundred years earlier.

The odd thing is that if King James had commandeered a document of Jacobean English, he would have found no difficulty in procuring a team of brilliant, if erratic, translators. There never was, I think, such good translation done as was done in England just before, during, and just after the seventeenth century. In 1611 North (of North's Plutarch) was dead; Urquhart and Motteux, the translators of Rabelais, L'Estrange, the translator of Josephus, were not yet available. But Florio (of Florio's Montaigne) was still alive; Philemon Holland was at the height of his amazing activity; Shelton was just preparing to start on *Don Quixote*. What a trio! Their version, I suspect, would not have lasted fifty years; it would have been diffuse, quaint, and not always accurate. But it

[1] 1 Cor. xiii. 1–7.

would have been splendid English of the period. And it is to those seven authors, and others like them, that I would direct the attention of any young man who wanted models for the translator to imitate. I would have him imitate them, not in their vocabulary, much of which is obsolete, nor in their conceits, which sometimes impose themselves unseasonably; but in their determination to *write*, to produce a work of art, not a mere transcript of foreign phrases and foreign idioms, set out under the dastardly apology, "Well, that's what it says!"

They have been accused, these people, of sitting too loose to their originals. Thus, Charles Whibley writes of Holland:

> His was not the ingenuity which would echo a foreign phrase in native English, and, tried by the standard of perfect consonance, his translations fail of their effect. He did not put Livy and Suetonius in an appropriate dress; rather, he took Suetonius or Livy, and tricked them out in the garb of his own time. So that he gives us . . . a quick vision of Livy or Suetonius had they been born in Elizabethan England.[1]

That criticism seems to me greatly exaggerated; and in so far as it is not exaggerated, I doubt whether it ought to be regarded as a criticism. Listen to Holland's rendering of the paragraph in Pliny's *Natural History*[2] which describes the river Jordan:

> A pleasant river it is, and as the site of the country will permit and give leave, winding and turning in and out, seeking as it were for love and honour, and applying itself to please the neighbour inhabitants. Full against his will, as it were, he passeth to the Lake of Sodom, Asphaltitis, and is swallowed up of it, where amongst those pestilent and

[1] Introduction to Holland's Suetonius, in Tudor Translations, p. xx.
[2] v, 15.

42

deadly waters, he loseth his own, that are so good and wholesome. And therefore, to keep himself out of it as long as he possibly could, upon the first opportunity of any valleys, he maketh a lake, which many call Genesara.

And the tradition persists. Roger L'Estrange was only a schoolboy when Holland died; yet here is another expert in making the Classics readable. This is his account of the portents recorded by Josephus[1] as foreshadowing the fall of Jerusalem:

> Some short time after the festival was over, on the twenty-first of the month Artemisius, there appeared a prodigy of a vision so extraordinary, that I should hardly venture to repeat it, if I could not produce several eyewitnesses that are yet living to confirm the truth of it. There were seen up and down in the air, before sunset, chariots and armed men all over the country, passing along with the clouds round about the city. Upon the feast of Pentecost, as the priests were a-going to officiate in the Temple according to custom, they heard at first a kind of confused murmur; and after that, a voice calling out earnestly in articulate words, *Let us be gone, let us be gone.*

You do not think either of Pliny or of Josephus as an inspired author, and yet how they come to life, these men of a silver age, under the translator's golden wand!

May I pursue the fortunes of English prose translation before we consider the fate of verse? That will be, after all, to follow the order of our inquiry; it is chiefly in prose that we ask whether the rendering is sufficiently literal; chiefly in verse that we ask whether the translator has preserved the style and idiom of his original. I do not know any better description of the change introduced by the polite affectations of the

[1] *Jewish War*, vii, 12.

eighteenth century than that given by George Wyndham in his introduction to North's Plutarch.[1] He is considering first North's translation—or rather, as we know, North's translation of Amyot's French translation; then the edition produced in 1683 by one of Dryden's ghosts, with a preface by Dryden himself; then the standard translation, issued by the Langhornes in 1770; and finally some version by a modern scholar who is left charitably anonymous. Here is his verdict:

> It was a colossal impertinence to put out *The Lives* among the Greeklings of Grub Street . . . but it must be noted that this, after North's, is the only version that can be read without impatience. Dryden's hacks were not artists, but neither were they prigs . . . and if they missed the rapture of sixteenth-century rhythm, they had not bleached the colour, carded the texture, and ironed the surface of their language to the well-glazed insignificance of the later eighteenth century. Their Plutarch is no longer arrayed in the royal robes of Amyot and North, but he is spared the cheap though formal tailoring of . . . the Langhornes. . . . In our own time, there have been translations by scholars; they are useful as cribs, but do not pretend to charm.

It died hard, the Elizabethan tradition; Melmoth, whom we only remember because Dr. Johnson in some dispute "reduced him to a whistle",[2] was still translating Cicero's letters and Pliny's in the old, racy fashion. But the Palladian curtain was descending on our literature: everywhere, Tudor brick was being refaced with Georgian ashlar. The new renderings were perhaps more accurate than the old, but terribly dead and stylized. Worse was to come in the nineteenth century: and, I am sorry to say, under the influence of religion. The

---

[1] Preface to North's Plutarch in Tudor Translations, p. lxxx.
[2] Boswell's *Life*, letter of 1 May 1780.

Oxford Movement aroused, from the first, a fresh interest in the writings of the Fathers; in these times of acute controversy they must be made available even to minds which had little tincture of scholarship. As its influence grew it produced a demand for English editions of the great spiritual classics: St. John of the Cross, St. Theresa, St. Francis of Sales, and the rest of them. I would not be controversial; equal blame, I think, attaches to the men who went with Newman and to the men who stayed behind with Pusey; the fact, as I see it, is that where religion is concerned our standard of translation has been, and remains, miserably low. Literalness has been accepted as our rule, and dullness is the result.

I will not entertain you—I might easily—with choice specimens of really stuffed-owl renderings in this field; such as that famous translation from the Italian, about the medieval story of a woman who was turned into a horse: "Her husband, distressed beyond measure at this melancholy event, the more so as the wretched creature refused all food, whether of men or animals", and so on. I will be content to read you a short passage from St. Cyril, in the Library of the Fathers:[1]

> For who has now brought thee to this assembly? What soldiers? With what bonds hast thou been forced? What doom has driven thee here now? No, but the salutary trophy of Jesus, the Cross, has brought you all together. This has enslaved the Persians, and tamed the Scythians; this to the Egyptians has given, for cats and dogs and their manifold errors, the knowledge of God; this, to this day, heals diseases; this, to this day, drives away devils, and overthrows the juggleries of drugs and charms.

Now, this is not too bad; it is at least intelligible; but how it gives itself away, at every turn, as a translation! And yet it was Newman who edited the series, and the actual translator

[1] *Catechetical Lectures*, xiii, 40.

was a divine of that day who counts next to Newman as an English stylist, Dean Church. Why didn't he make a better job of it? I think he, and others like him, unconsciously assumed that all holy books ought to be translated literally, because the Bible was such a success when it was translated literally; it was a tribute we owed to the sacred character of the documents. And the result has been disastrous. They remain inaccessible to the ordinary Englishman, the chaste Latinity of St. Leo, the tireless rhetoric of St. Augustine, the splendid declamations of Bossuet and Lacordaire—and so much else!

In our own day the need for good, readable translations is greater than ever. On the one hand, only a tiny percentage of us is capable of reading the Classics. On the other hand we have become, in these last fifty years, more European; we are more interested than our forefathers in the doings and sayings of foreigners. We must not underestimate the achievements of the present century; a century in which Gilbert Murray has put Euripides across our English footlights, and Charles Scott-Moncrieff has beguiled us into the impression that we have read Proust. But our general standard is still hopelessly pedestrian. There has been a vast output of classical translations by scholars, but was George Wyndham wrong in describing them as "cribs"? A great scholar is not necessarily a great master of English; his ear is too much haunted by echoes of classical phrase and idiom to be in tune with the taste of the common man. Or how is it that a humanist like John Phillimore could disfigure (for me) his edition of Propertius by continually rendering *mea puella* "my girl"? And as for our translations from modern languages, you will light upon one here and there which has been competently done, but for the most part your publisher has fallen back on the assistance of maiden ladies who have travelled abroad, and have just learned not to split their infinitives. Thus, in what I take to be a

standard edition of *The Three Musketeers* (translator anonymous),
you will come across the phrase, "The devil! What you say
there is very sad"[1]—a formula which may be good Poirot, but
is certainly not good English. For my own part, I do not see
that anything can be done about it until we get rid of this false
tradition, until we get back to the Jacobean instinct of putting
literature first, and literalness second.

It is time we considered the other question under dispute
—Can the translator rest content when he has expressed the
meaning of his original? Or is he bound—especially when
dealing with poetry—to convey something of the style and
idiom of his original? Is the process involved merely like that
of giving exchange for a sum of money in a foreign currency?
Or is it like that of transposing a piece of music from one key
to another? There are, of course, exceptional cases in which
the form of your original has an importance not to be overlooked. As, for example, when you are translating a song or a
hymn which is to be sung in English to the same tune; or when
the point of the passage depends (for instance, where Daniel
gives judgement in the Story of Susanna) on word-play. I
would add, although I know I shall be charged with per-
nicketiness, that an abecedarian original like the Lamentations
of Jeremiah deserves an abecedarian rendering. But these are
special cases; what is the ordinary rule to be observed? Professor Newman, in the introduction to that version of Homer
which was so mercilessly attacked by Matthew Arnold, announces his intention of retaining every peculiarity of the
original, with the greater care the more foreign it may happen
to be; so that it may never be forgotten that he is imitating,
and imitating in a different material.[2] Dryden's principle is
quite different: "I have endeavoured to make Virgil speak
such English as he himself would have spoken, if he had been

[1] Warne & Co., New York, ch. 26.
[2] Arnold's lectures *On Translating Homer*, p. 2.

born in England, and in this present age."[1] If you take Newman's principle too seriously, you raise a doubt whether
translation, in the strict sense, is possible at all. This is the
argument of Sir Edward Cook:[2] "Nothing is really fine poetry
unless it will make sense when translated into prose." (He
was writing in 1919.) "Nothing is really fine poetry unless
the value of it disappears when translated into prose." And
Professor Bradley[3] seems to have been of the same opinion; if
he translates a line of Virgil, "And were stretching forth their
hands in longing for the further bank", the charm of the
original, he tells us, has fled. "Why has it fled?" (he con-
tinues). "Because I have changed the *meaning* of Virgil's line.
What that meaning is, I cannot say; Virgil has said it."

Let us take up that point first—the possibility of adequate
translation. There may be lines here and there, in Virgil
especially, which defy a just rendering; that is only to say that
the translator, here and there, has to throw up the sponge in
a footnote. We must not despair of taking even Virgil at high
tide, just because of that seventh wave that leaps curling over
the sea-front. No, translation is possible, and translation without any loss. I am driven to prove that by an example; it is
easiest to take an example known to all of you; yet I beg
leave to quote it in full, lest I should seem to be deriving
an unfair advantage from weak memories. It will serve my
turn, William Johnson Cory's rendering of the Heraclitus
epigram—[4]

They told me, Heraclitus, they told me you were dead;
They brought me bitter news to hear, and bitter tears to
    shed;
I wept as I remembered how often you and I
Had tired the sun with talking, and sent him down the sky.

[1] Preface to the *Aeneid*.
[2] *More Literary Recreations*, p. 170.
[3] Quoted by J. Lewis May in the *Tablet*, 25 March 1957.
[4] See Johnson's *Ionica*; Call., *Ep.* 47.

And now that thou art lying, my dear old Carian guest,
A handful of grey ashes, long, long ago at rest,
Still are thy pleasant voices, thy nightingales, awake;
For death, he taketh all away, but them he cannot take.

I am not suggesting that that is a perfect piece of English
poetry. But then, I don't think Callimachus' original is a
perfect specimen of Greek poetry. If you like we will call it
a good beta-double-plus version of a good beta-double-plus
original. Cory has put in nothing which is not there, at least
germinally, in the Greek. He has left nothing out except one
rather disconcerting particle. The metre he uses is not anything like the elegiac metre; but he has contrived to give us an
English substitute which produces the same nostalgic effect as
Greek elegiacs. He is stirring at the back of our minds an
unconscious echo of Hood's poem:

I remember, I remember, the house where I was born;
The little window where the sun came peeping in at
morn.

That is translation. If you did not know your Greek anthology,
you would willingly accept the result as an original poem by
the author of *Mimnermus in Church*.

Lord Woodhouselee, in his essay on the *Principles of Translation* (a valuable book, published near the end of the eighteenth century), is something of a precisian. "Next in importance to a faithful transfusion of the sense and meaning of
an author, is the assimilation of the style and manner of
writing in the translation to that of the original." And, after
several chapters giving examples of failure and success in this
particular, he adds, "We may certainly, from the foregoing
observations, conclude that it is impossible to do complete
justice to any species of poetical composition in a prose translation; in other words, that none but a poet can translate a

poet.''[1] Personally, whatever the truth about the principle he lays down, I should not admit the inference he draws from it. If we are right in insisting that a good translation should have the freshness of an original product, then surely, at this point in the argument, we should take the length and solidity of a given poem into account before we say that you cannot make prose of it. Mackail's renderings from the Greek Anthology are lovely renderings, but they are not the sort of stuff an Englishman would commit to paper. The same may be said of Horace's odes, so fugitive, often so rambling; may be said, I think, of most elegiac writing—the clandestine amours of first-century Rome become a sorry business when you write them down in cold blood; they do not stand on their own legs as a piece of essay-writing. On the other hand a play (though the Greek choruses provide an obvious difficulty) does not need the aid of poetry to carry it off. And where you are dealing with an epic, I would claim that you may make your choice freely. The *Iliad* might have been written in prose, like the *Morte d'Arthur*. The *Odyssey* might have been written in prose, like *Baron Munchhausen*. In recent times—perhaps the success of Butcher and Lang had something to do with it— the choice remains open. Two contemporaries of my own, T. E. Lawrence and Dr. Rieu, have given us a prose *Odyssey*; but Mr. Day Lewis found a rather loose metrical scheme appropriate to the *Aeneid*, and Miss Sayers is translating Dante in *terza rima*—the third such rendering published within thirty years.

The older translators gave us verse for verse. What incredible people they were, the men of Shakespeare's time! Sir John Harington was told by Queen Elizabeth to produce an English version of the *Orlando Furioso*, and he sat down and did it; though he admits, with the effrontery of his age, that he has cut down Ariosto's cantos ''by omitting many staves

[1] Pages 63 and 111 in the Everyman edition.

of them, and sometimes put the matter of two or three staves into one".[1] And it is all astonishingly competent; pursue the drowsy narrative for a page or two, and you would swear you were reading Spenser. They are all competent, these people, except "Leviathan" Hobbes, whose grey hairs were dishonoured by a villainous translation of Homer. Yet who, nowadays, reads Marlowe's Lucan? Only Chapman survives, through the accident of Keats' writing a sonnet about him; and the effect on the modern reader is less than astronomical. For myself, I confess, Chapman hangs fire. All these early achievements were eclipsed by two translations which, be they what they may, are poetry of the first order, Dryden's Virgil and Pope's Homer.

Poetry of the first order; are they translations of the first order? Where they fail, it is precisely over the point we are discussing; instead of preserving, in any recognizable way, the idiom of the original, they force an idiom on the original. It is surely a suspicious circumstance that Homer, once he has passed through the mangle of the heroic couplet, comes out exactly like Virgil! If we had had three more such poets the whole of literature would have been digested into heroics. And not only classical or foreign literature; witness Dryden's up-to-date version of *The Knight's Tale*:

> He through a little window cast his sight,
> Through thick of bars, that gave a scanty light;
> But even that glimmering served him to descry
> The inevitable charms of Emily . . . [2]

Chaucer, beyond doubt, has suffered a sea-change; and has Virgil really fared better? The attempt to impose a single formula on all literature was bound to defeat itself. Nor is the heroic couplet, with its indispensable punch at the end of each second verse, an apt vehicle for the sprawling effects of the

[1] Last page but one in the preface (edition of 1607).   [2] Lines 229-32.

epic. For the modern reader it involves an additional embarrassment. Ever since Martinus Scriblerus we have been conscious how easy it is for the heroic couplet to fall, and how disastrous is the fall of it; we are ever anxious for the poet, and when Pope, innocently enough, gives you the couplet,[1]

> But when old age had dimmed Lycurgus' eyes,
> To Ereuthalion he consigned the prize,

it stirs a memory of *Rejected Addresses*,

> But when John Dwyer 'listed in the Blues
> Emmanuel Jennings polished Stubbs's shoes.[2]

We are like men watching a tight-rope performance; sure that the acrobat will not really stumble, yet consumed with apprehension that he *might*.

From the first, Pope and Dryden were criticized because they missed the feeling and force of the original. Pope's rendering of Sarpedon's speech to Glaucus[3] has justly been quoted as a splendid piece of writing; but it does not culminate in the ἴομεν which Carteret immortalized on his death-bed. And so it is with most of the great lines in Virgil. "Trust not their presents, nor admit the horse" will pass muster in the context, but you cannot quote it as a substitute for *timeo Danaos et dona ferentes*.[4] And there is much ingenuity in the lines:

> Even the mute walls relate the warrior's fame,
> And Trojan griefs the Tyrian's pity claim—

but it is not quite *sunt lacrimae rerum*.[5] Meanwhile, what dethroned Pope and Dryden was not a mere return to accuracy. It was that revolt against the Palladian and the classical which we call the Romantic Revival. New experiments were being

[1] *Iliad*, vii, 148. [2] *The Theatre*, by the Revd. G. C.
[3] *Iliad*, xii, 310–28. [4] *Aeneid*, ii, 49.
[5] *Aeneid*, i, 462.

tried in the earlier part of the nineteenth century, by way of presenting the Classics in a form more English, and perhaps (as we say nowadays) more "folk". Matthew Arnold was already criticizing this tendency in the sixties; he had not yet been confronted with William Morris's *Odyssey*, in which the hero is no longer described as the destroyer of cities, but as the Burg-bane: in which Nausicaa, faced with the necessity of washing her brothers' evening shirts, is made to complain,

> And ever will they be having new-washed weed, forsooth,
> When to the dance they wend them.[1]

Evidently there was the danger that we should slip back into the eighteenth-century error of forcing our own idiom—a Nordic one, this time—on the authors of antiquity. The Victorian Age has left behind it some notable pieces of translation, such as Butcher and Lang's *Odyssey*, and Conington's *Aeneid*. But even in such writing the modern ear is quick to detect a hint of fustian. *Quisque suos patimur manes*, Virgil may have written; but why should he be saddled with the *manes* of Sir Walter Scott?

In our own day, the tide of fashion has set in very differently. We are prepared to translate anything, the Classics included, into current English speech. And this makes it more urgent than ever that we should find an answer to our second question, Is the translator bound to reproduce the style and idiom of his original? We ask ourselves whether it is possible to give a plausible rendering of (say) Herodotus in modern phrase without spoiling the effect of his *naïveté*. Can we be content merely to reproduce his meaning? If I may presume to dogmatize about this, I would suggest that in the long run the meaning is what matters—if under the word "meaning" you include emphasis. There could be no better illustration of a false emphasis than the opening of Dryden's *Eclogues*:

[1] *Odyssey*, vi, 64.

> Beneath the shade which beechen boughs diffuse,
> You, Tityrus, entertain your silvan Muse;
> Round the wide world in banishment we roam,
> Forced from our pleasing fields, and native home.

The whole point of the sentence in Virgil is the contrast between the good luck Tityrus has had and the bad luck Meliboeus has had; a contrast which disappears completely in the translation. Meaning and emphasis must be preserved, but we are not bound to imitate tricks of manner. There is nothing really to be said for rendering the *Iliad* in English hexameters, as Matthew Arnold wanted to. There is no reason to use long sentences in your translation because your author (Cicero, for example) uses long sentences. There is no harm in subordinating your sentences where your author—the Book of Proverbs, for example—is content to co-ordinate them. You are under contract to give, not an imitation, but the equivalent of your original; that is the point.

But when we have said that, we have not quite said everything. A good translation does not demand a mechanical reproduction of detail; but it does demand a certain identity of atmosphere. Mr. Day Lewis has said a wise word on this subject: "To catch the tone of your original, there must be some sort of affinity between you and him." Without this, "you cannot reach through the words and thoughts of your original, and make contact with the man who wrote it".[1] Woodhouselee puts it even more strongly when he tells us that the translator "must adopt the very soul of his author, which must speak through his organs".[2] He must, in fact, get inside somebody else's skin before he undertakes the rendering of a single sentence. This is not always easy; I myself am committed at the moment to the autobiography of St. Theresa of Lisieux. It is not a simple process to put yourself inside

---

[1] Introduction to the *Aeneid*, p. ix.   [2] Op. cit., p. 114.

the skin of a young French female saint. But you have got, somehow, to sink your own personality and wrap yourself round in a mood, whenever you sit down at your writing-table for such work as this. All translation is a kind of impersonation; make a success of that, and style and idiom will follow.

It is, I think, absence of that *rapport* between author and translator that has wrecked T. E. Lawrence's version of the *Odyssey*. He was brought up, as we were all brought up fifty years ago, to suppose that the *Odyssey* is of much later date than the *Iliad*, the work of an imitator. He announces, therefore, that he is going to give us a Wardour Street rendering of a Wardour Street original. But he does not really sustain this pose, and the result is patchy and unconvincing. He has not put himself inside Homer's skin. Whereas Dr. Rieu, who is modern enough to accept the unity of Homer, puts on no critical airs, does not waste time in dogmatizing about the sort of person Homer must have been; he just throws himself into the story. I picture him as a schoolmaster addressing a set of senior boys with the formula, "Look here, let's pretend I'm Homer. I'm going to tell you some jolly good yarns."

There may be fresh changes in public taste lying ahead of us. But, as things are, I would recommend the translator to write modern English, if he is concerned with a document of any length—as long, say, as the *Tome* of St. Leo or the *Pensées* of Pascal. The Victorians could take it; they could feel at home in Burton's *Arabian Nights* in spite of a sentence like "Sore waxed my cark and my care, for I kenned that there remained to me of life but the morrow". We are less patient of pastiche; one night is all very well, but we shrink from a thousand more of this kind of thing. And, if we are to write modern English, "thou" has to go, with all the verbal forms appropriate to it, except in translation designed for liturgical use. Take the *Imitation of Christ*; I only know one edition, and that quite recent, which renders the second person singular by "you" and "yours". And yet the *Imitation of Christ* is not essentially a late medieval document: the spiritual situations it deals with are those of our own day. If it is to have a direct impact on the conscience it must convey its message under the unlovely American formula, "This means you!" The effect is lost, somehow, if we substitute the locution, "This meaneth thee".

To write modern English is not, believe me, a soft option; on the whole, it is much more difficult than writing pastiche. You need continual watchfulness and self-discipline, especially when you are aiming at an effect of great simplicity. Dr. Rieu sometimes nods in his excellent rendering of the *Odyssey*; a phrase like "with a liberal donation from my booty" has more than a hint of journalese; on the other hand, when he writes, "laden with the pick of the Argive chivalry bringing doom and slaughter to the Trojans", he is slipping back, without noticing it, into Butcher and Lang.[1] But above all, we are faced with the question whether writing modern English involves the use of colloquialism, and what is the dividing line between colloquialism and *argot*. I confess that I have my hesitations about slang, except, of course, when you are dealing with an author like Aristophanes or Plautus. The trouble is its impermanence. Miss Sayers, in her introduction to the *Inferno*,[2] mentions a particular line in which she was faced with a choice between,

> Master, this prospect likes me not a whit,

and,

> Sir, I don't like the looks of this one bit.

Now, I quite agree with Miss Sayers that Dante himself writes at different levels; he is not, consistently, what Matthew Arnold would call "noble". But the locution "one bit" is very modern indeed; have we any guarantee that in twenty or

[1] See pages 215 and 138 (Penguin edition).
[2] p. 61, referring to xxi, 127 in the poem.

thirty years it will not be dated? So it is when Jowett makes Thrasymachus refer to Socrates and his friends as "silly-billies",[1] a word unknown nowadays outside the nursery: or when Sir Edward Marsh credits Horace with the sentiment,

Now we'll go berserk—let the binge begin,[2]

a line which rings in my ears as nostalgically Edwardian. So, when Aeneas is tempted to kill Helen, on the last night of Troy, Mr. Day Lewis has the phrase, "Was she going to get away with it?" Admirable; it rings the bell. But was not this, too, perhaps a temptation? The translator must always look fifty years ahead.

Not that you can really do that. Current English is current in more senses than one, and nobody can possibly tell you what it will be like in A.D. 2007. Consider a phrase which appeared recently in *The Times* newspaper,[3] "Staggering, in this sense of ironing out or levelling up or removing a bottle-neck"—what would John Ruskin have said to such an *obscurum per obscurius*? Nor do the idioms of the language remain fixed, any more than its vocabulary. How often have we been told that "inversion"—putting a word out of its natural place in the sentence, by way of emphasizing it—is quite obsolete? Yet we have all grown accustomed to sentences like "Prominent among the supporters of the bill is dark-haired, fifty-year-old Mr. Higgins". Oh for a timeless English! The translator must do his best by using the speech that comes natural to him, fortified a little by those good old English words which are out of favour, but not obsolete. His style must be his own, his rhetoric and his emphasis must be that of his original. And always, at the back of his mind, he must imagine that he is the original.

Can he hope, in any case, that his version will live? At least, if he does his work well, he will have the comfort of

---

[1] *Republic*, 336 c.   [2] *Odes*, iii, 19.   [3] 20 March 1957.

being pirated by his successors. The standard edition of *Don Quixote*, published with the Doré illustrations in the late eighteen-sixties, was a cento of two earlier versions more than a century old—one of them, by Motteux, dating back to 1719. Only, he must be a craftsman. The publisher, having paid something (in the case of a modern foreign book) to the author, wants the rendering done by a hack. But you cannot get craftsmanship for £200 down. How numerous, nowadays, are the retired men of distinction who would like to solace their declining years with the grateful labour of translation; the poets and novelists who have written themselves out, and would be better employed in such work than in turning out shallow volumes of criticism! But there is no inducement. If the inducement were there, and if the candidates were hand-picked after submitting specimens of their work, I believe we might hope, not unreasonably, to enter upon a second Elizabethan age of English translation.

RICHARD CRASHAW

Spooner, who was Warden of New College at the beginning of the century—a man known to fame, but unjustly, for I believe he never in his life perpetrated a Spoonerism —was once asked whether there was much Christian Socialism in Oxford. His reply was, "No, I shouldn't say there was much; in fact, I think there are only two Christian Socialists in Oxford, Dr. Rashdall and myself." (Dr. Rashdall, afterwards Dean of Carlisle, was a clerical Fellow of New College.) "Only Dr. Rashdall and myself; and I'm not very much of a Socialist, and Dr. Rashdall isn't very much of a Christian." In the same way, if you asked a rather forgetful person whether there were any great religious poets in England during the first half of the seventeenth century, he would be apt to reply, "Only two, Donne and Herbert; and Herbert wasn't a very great poet, and Donne wasn't very religious." Then, after a moment's pause, he would add, "Oh, I'd forgotten Crashaw."

Comparisons are odious, but they are also illuminating. Donne, Herbert and Crashaw form a remarkable triad; nor is the number complete—Herrick, too, was a poet of that age, and Herrick, like the others, was a clergyman. Herbert was unquestionably a religious man, but I don't think he was more than a moderate poet. What appeals to me in Herbert is quaintness, rather than grandeur. Donne was a great poet, greater, perhaps, than Crashaw, but I don't think he was, fundamentally, a religious man. Herrick is questionable on both grounds. You may, nevertheless, think him a religious man and a great poet into the bargain. But even so, I would not class him with Crashaw. His fame depends chiefly on what he himself called his "unbaptized numbers"; and even his devotional writings lack depth. Whereas Crashaw's poetry was all religion, and Crashaw's religion was all poetry. Unlike Donne, unlike Herrick, he is fully integrated.

Let me amplify that a little, or I may seem to be dismissing great names too summarily. You can't help liking George Herbert, even if your appreciation only takes the form of thinking he was a dear old gentleman. (Actually he was forty when he died.) But he is one of your safe candidates; he takes no risks, he doesn't aspire to the heights. Of his piety there is no question, and sometimes he rings the bell by achieving a happy phrase, polished and quotable. But you don't (at least I don't) come across things in his works which make you say to yourself aloud, "By Gad, that's good!" Herrick has a cleverness which sometimes makes him run with Crashaw for the length of an epigram, but when all is said and done, he has very little to tell us about religion. It would be too harsh to say that he was only a parson on Sundays, but the *Hesperides* do outnumber the *Noble Numbers* by five to one; he is such a humanist, so easily distracted by every trivial thought which comes along, that you do not really picture him as a man of prayer. With Donne the case is worse; he is a man morbidly preoccupied with sex. No, not just the comfortable grossness of the Jacobean age; I am sure Donne's psyche was all wrong —look at that extraordinary poem about the flea! To be sure, he was a theologian; he has been called the last of the schoolmen; and I suppose that is why Johnson, so inappropriately, labelled this whole group of poets "metaphysical". But (to my mind) he writes of sacred subjects with a marble detachment; how complimentary he is to the Virgins in his Litany! Turn from that to his essay on Virginity, and it makes a hypocrite of him at once. With Donne, as with Milton, you feel that he was a man much interested in religion, but not a religious man.

With Crashaw, it is just the other way; we really know nothing about him, except what belongs to a religious context. The story of his life can be told in a sentence; that he was a much-loved Fellow of Peterhouse, the friend of Cowley, that he was ejected by the Puritans, became a Catholic, went abroad, was given a minor benefice at Loreto, and died there when he had been in enjoyment of it for a few weeks. Turn to his writings to fill out the picture, and you will find that he only produced about fifty poems on secular subjects, and ten of these were epitaphs; the man who aspired to live a dying life has bequeathed to us a thanatography, rather than a biography. There is nothing about love-affairs, nothing about quarrels, nothing about pets, nothing about May-day revelry or hay-making or getting drunk; the whole stock-in-trade of his literary contemporaries seems to have passed him by.

The anonymous preface to the first edition of *Steps to the Temple* has seized upon this characteristic, and perhaps made too much of it. "It were profane", says this unknown editor, "but to mention here in the preface those under-headed poets, retainers to seven shares and a half, whose only business in verse is to rhyme a poor sixpenny soul, a suburb sinner, into hell. . . . [I have no idea what those phrases mean] Oh, when the general arraignment of poets shall be . . . with what a triumphant brow shall our poet sit above, and look down upon poor Homer, Virgil, Horace, Claudian etc.; who had amongst them the ill luck to talk out a great part of their gallant genius upon bees, dung, frogs, and gnats etc., and not as himself here, upon scriptures, divine graces, martyrs and angels!" This might seem to suggest that Crashaw was a Puritan or an exquisite, who turned away from base subjects as unworthy of him. I doubt if it was that; I think he simply hadn't the itch to write a poem about everything he came across. Imagine the four poets going for a walk together and passing, say, a scarecrow. Donne would have been reminded of his Classics;

let us hope that he would have remained silent. Herrick would have turned out some graceful little couplet that didn't get you anywhere, as, for instance:

> Look, Stranger, on this Scar-crow! And see what
> Panique he spreads on all sides, having my hat.

George Herbert would have thought out a longish poem on obvious lines, about the Cross scaring away Divells. But I don't think it would have occurred to Crashaw that there was anything to write about. He was too introverted, I suspect, to have his themes forced upon him by outward encounter.

What was it, then, that set Crashaw a-rhyming? Undoubtedly, I think, the influence of the Latin classics. When we have given up reading the Classics altogether, in forty or fifty years' time, I do not see how people will begin to understand the nature or the inspiration of Jacobean poetry. Shut your eyes, and imagine yourself in a library that has its basis, as a library should, in the well-printed, well-bound editions of the early seventeenth century. What are the names that leap to your mind? Ovid, yes, and Martial. Lose sight of those two, and the technique of Jacobean poetry becomes, at once, unintelligible. Let me indulge in a few generalizations, obvious enough, and incomplete as generalizations always are. The genius of the Latin language is capable of being developed in two different directions. There is the sonorous, rhetorical tradition of Cicero and Virgil. There is the concentrated, epigrammatic tradition of Tacitus and Martial. The latter is the inspiration of the Jacobeans, with their intense verbal cleverness, their allusive silences, their striving after paradox. The other, the rhetorical tradition, was Milton's choice; Virgil was his parent, or if you will his grandparent, with Dante as the intervening generation. His choice won; Dryden and Pope carried on the Virgilian tradition, though with a slight difference which is, in a way, the analogue of Lucan.

Lucan, with his "victrix causa deis placuit, sed victa Catoni", his "nil actum credens, dum quid superesset agendum"; it is Virgil, but more formalized, more neatly tied up at the edges. And what Lucan did to Virgil, Dryden, in a way, did to Milton. It was Latin in the grand manner; they had left behind them the mere cleverness, and the somewhat crabbed restraint, of Tacitus and Martial and the Jacobeans.

Tacitus and Martial, I say, but the discoverer of the vein was Ovid. It was from Ovid, surely, that they learned their love of conceits; of singling out one incongruous feature in a situation, and either throwing it into violent relief by the shock tactics of an epigram, or else worrying it slowly to death under a series of alternative images. An excellent example of the latter method is to be found in Crashaw's "Invitation", addressed to Lady Denbigh when she could not quite make up her mind to become a Catholic. The incongruity of the situation, familiar to all who have been through the experience, is that you reach a point at which your mind is convinced but your will remains irresolute. That is Crashaw's opportunity:

> What magic bolts, what mystic bars
> Maintain the will in these strange wars?
> What fatal yet fantastic bands
> Keep the free heart from its own hands?
> So, when the year takes cold, we see
> Poor waters their own prisoners be;
> Fettered, and locked up fast they lie
> In a sad self-captivity;
> The astonished nymphs their flood's strange fate deplore,
> To see themselves their own severer shore.

How Ovidian that poem is, I have reason to know, because I amused myself by turning the whole of it into elegiacs thirty years ago, when I was in the Countess of Denbigh's position myself. You do not really understand a poem until you have

63

turned it into Latin verse. And this one, believe me, simply fell into the Ovidian formula.

But Crashaw's first efforts were based on Martial, not on Ovid. His *Epigrammata Sacra* were printed by the Cambridge University Press in 1634; it was the only one of his books he ever saw through the press himself; the rest were published for him by friends when he was already in exile. Here you have a Fellow of Peterhouse, whose mind is saturated, as the minds of dons were in those happier days, with the Classics. He is, besides, a man of deep religious feeling. He is inclined to model himself on George Herbert, a friend, like himself, of the Little Gidding circle, for whom he has a profound admiration. (*The Temple* appeared in the year immediately before *Epigrammata Sacra*.) As he thumbs his Gospels, and meditates on them, Crashaw gets certain "lights" as we all do; he seizes, for the first time, the full point of some utterance of our Lord's, notices, for the first time, some happy coincidence which links this occurrence, undesignedly, with that. The ordinary Christian's instinct is to make a note of the circumstance in some common-place book, some journal of retreat; the ordinary clergyman's instinct is to lay it up as the text for a sermon. Crashaw's instinct is somewhat different. He crystallizes his thought in the form of an English, or more probably of a Latin, epigram.

Do not be too ready to exclaim at the cold-bloodedness of the proceeding. The man, remember, thinks as easily in Latin as in English; cannot be sure, until he turns back and questions his own thought, whether he is thinking in Latin or in English. Many of the sacred epigrams were printed in both languages, and it is an amusing game to speculate, in any given case, which form was the original. An amusing game, but I don't think you will often find yourself able to pronounce with certainty. And remember that paradox, to the Christian thinker, is not an intellectual exercise, far-fetched, cultivated with laborious ingenuity. It is a sort of open-cast mining, to look for paradox in the Gospels. After all, if the thing is true; if God did lie in a stable, if the Eternal did die on a cross, the paradox is there, hitting you in the eye—you cannot get away from it. Or again, if you live in a fallen world with a fallen nature, perpetually in love with a moral ideal which you find yourself incapable of achieving, it does not need a Crashaw to find paradox in the situation; St. Paul himself will tell you, "What I do is not what I wish to do, but something which I hate." *Odi et amo*—it takes you straight back to Catullus.

The patentee of commenting on the Gospels by epigram is St. Augustine. He had inherited, through Tertullian, the tradition of prose-fireworks which came down from Tacitus, and there was no word he commented on but might set him off on a full tide of paradox. Listen to him on the word *fatigatus*, when our Lord sits down wearied at the well of Samaria. "Not for nothing is he wearied, he, who is God's strength; not for nothing is he wearied, he, who gives the weary rest; not for nothing is he wearied, he, whose absence makes us so feeble, whose presence makes us so strong . . . Christ's power it was that created thee; it needed Christ's weakness to re-create thee." Notice the pun on the word "recreation"; it is characteristic of the style. "Through Christ's power, the nothing thou wast came to be; but for Christ's weakness, the being thou hadst had passed into nothing. His power fashioned us; it was his weakness that came to find us, when we were lost." All that (and much more) is St. Augustine's commentary on one word. And must Crashaw never let himself go, when the same opportunity lay before him?

He did let himself go; not on any principle, it would seem, but whenever a point happened to strike him. Take, as a sample of this style, what was perhaps the best poem he wrote in this style, his well-known epigram on the Widow's Mite.

The *Epigrammata Sacra*, as they were published in 1634, were all in Latin; let us be content with the English version which he published later—and perhaps composed earlier.

> Two mites, two drops—yet all her house and land,
> Fall from a steady heart, though trembling hand;
> The others' wanton wealth foams high and brave;
> The other cast away, she only gave.

That is as good an epigram as you would get anywhere; yet, observe, it does not go a step beyond our Lord's own meaning. It only elaborates the contrast. If that is so (we are tempted to ask), why not be content with our Lord's own words? The objection is ill found; to have restated the meaning of a Gospel passage first in your own Latin, then in your own English, is in a sense to have mastered it. The artist cannot be content with gazing at the face he loves, he must paint a portrait of it, to make it his own; so your poet, whose trade is in words, must translate the admired sentiment into his own language, so as to get outside it. Gospel text, and Crashaw's Latin, and Crashaw's English; here is a three-fold lock, to keep the treasure safe, like those old chests that could only be opened by the rector and both the churchwardens. Or is that fanciful? Have I been reading too much George Herbert?

That, surely, was the genesis of the *Epigrammata Sacra*; they are merely Crashaw rising from his knees in soliloquy. I dare swear that the Fellows of Peterhouse had plenty of ado to make him publish. The preface indicates that his friends had been prepared to underwrite the success of the book at their own risk. It also contains a very curious hint that the Jesuits will not be too pleased at its publication; it is very difficult to see why they should have minded. These are the qualms of self-consciousness; in downright fact there was little reason why anybody should have regretted the appearance of the book, or for that matter vociferously welcomed it. The formula becomes almost monotonous; echoes of the Augustinian paradox are ingeniously awoken at each successive stage of our Lord's life. You read the lesson of Bethlehem in the words, *Illi non locus est, quo sine nec locus est*: "Space is none for him, without whom space could not be." The apostles called away from their nets are fish in Christ's net now; *Una salus nobis est potuisse capi*: "Caught we must contrive to be, or there is no escaping." The withered fig-tree congratulates itself, *Non possum autumno nobiliore frui*: "Never was an autumn brought such glory with it." Even more Augustinian is the comment on our Lord's silence before his judges: *Ille olim verbum qui dixit, et omnia fecit, verbum non dicens omnia nunc reficit.* Crashaw's own translation, not quite so happy, is: "O mighty nothing, unto thee, Nothing, we owe all things that be. God spake once when he all things made, He saved all when he nothing said. The world was made of nothing then; 'Tis made by nothing now again." That is the formula of the thing; Martial Christianized.

Already you may trace the symptoms of that over-subtlety, that straining after paradox, which was Crashaw's danger. It wasn't really necessary to make a sick man address St. Peter in the words, "Thy shadow's shadow shall be my light." On the other hand, Crashaw in his early manner is sometimes simple almost to the verge of tameness, as in the well-known lines on the "sepulchre in which man was never yet laid":

> How life and death in thee
> Agree!
> Thou hadst a Virgin womb
> And tomb.
> A Joseph did betroth
> Them both.

Herbert could have written that; and indeed, if the authorship were doubtful, I think it would be attributed to Herbert. But, simple or complicated, the work which Crashaw published in 1634 gave no definite promise that he would be a poet. Rather, an agile scholar who could Latinize for you gracefully, as dons did know how to Latinize before we invented the word "research". He would define the following of Christ as "ire in bonam crucem" without once looking round to see if you caught his allusion. Moreover, where religion was concerned, he had the seeing eye; he could pick out for you the vein of tragic irony that runs through the Gospels. But, a great poet? Hardly that! If he had died fifteen years earlier he would have been, at best, a legend of the combination-room.

When was it, then, and under what stimulus, that Crashaw became a poet? The simplest answer, perhaps, is that he never did. Not, I mean, in the sense of intending to be a poet, or even wanting to be a poet; not in the sense of writing poetry for poetry's sake. The mood only took him occasionally. When his friends died, he wrote epitaphs about them. When anything happened at Court—the birth of a new baby, for example—he celebrated it in the overdone manner of his time. On much rarer, all too rare occasions, he got up from his knees and sang to God.

It was in 1646, when he was already in exile, and only three years before he died, that an admiring friend brought out two volumes in one, *Steps to the Temple* and *The Delights of the Muses*. It was not complete; did not contain, for example, the letter to the Countess of Denbigh, or the second hymn to St. Theresa. But it contained the bulk of his work, and the bulk was—what? Only some hundred and thirty pages in a generously spaced edition. It is hardly the length of Gray, unquestionably the idlest of our poets. Not a large output, really, for a man of thirty-six or thirty-seven, who had enjoyed, till he was thirty, what was then the delicious retirement of a Cambridge combination-room. He could have written more, surely, if he had set his mind to it. . . . But I don't think he ever did set his mind to it. His mind was elsewhere.

We will dismiss his court poems with short comment; a glance is enough. They will prepare us for the fact, which is evident in far more serious contexts, that Crashaw had not much gift of self-criticism. For the most part, he prudently took refuge in Latin; and I am afraid that, unless Henrietta Maria was something of a Latinist, his addresses will have passed unread by the addressee. But when he ventures on the expression of his loyalty in English, he does badly where no English poet has ever done well. Scriblerus might have quoted, or invented, one of his couplets:

> War, Blood, and Death (names all averse from joy)
> Hear this! We have another bright-eyed Boy!

The sequel to it is even more painful:

> Then let the eastern world brag and be proud
> Of one coy Phoenix, while we have a brood,
> A brood of phoenixes; while we have brother
> And sister phoenixes, and still the mother!
> And may we long; long mayst thou live, to increase
> The house and family of phoenixes.

It is unbelievable, but alas, it is textual.

Of the epitaphs, one stands in a class by itself, that on the Husband and Wife who died together; it is in the anthologies. "Let them sleep on, let them sleep on, Till this stormy night be gone"—that has the authentic effect of the very finest poetry, of making you catch your breath without being able to understand why it has happened. The rest are well enough, but there is nothing to single them out as remarkable in that age of industrious tomb-building. Perhaps the best is a short one, on his old school-master, Dr. Brooke, nearly spoilt, but not quite, by its quaintness.

A Brooke, whose stream, so great, so good
~~Was loved, was honoured as a Flood,~~
Whose banks the Muses dwelt upon
More than their own Helicon,
Here at length hath gladly found
A quiet passage underground;
Meanwhile his loved banks, now dry
The Muses with their tears supply.

But all through the *Delights of the Muses*, neither author nor reader is fully at ease. You have the overmastering impression that it is Thalia's day out; Urania has come in to oblige, but she knows and you know that it is not "her place". Crashaw always exaggerates his images; that is all very well in a religious context, where the supernatural impinges on the natural plane. But it strikes a false note in the secular poems, even in the most serious of them. Bishop Andrewes, to be sure, was a very great man, and when you stand before his portrait you may, if you will, describe it as a shadow cast by a setting sun; that is a fine notion. But you must not go on to say that Bishop Andrewes' death "left the dim face of this dull hemisphere All one great eye, all drowned in one great tear"—you are getting too far away from the facts. Of course, one poem in this collection was destined to represent Crashaw in all the anthologies, the lines to his Supposed Mistress. But, however beautiful, surely they are something of a *tour de force*? It is like Trollope killing Mrs. Proudie; you feel somebody had bet him that he couldn't do it.

It may be interpreted, still more significantly, as a gesture; a gesture of celibacy. It was an age of courtly love, by which I mean that you cannot imagine Herrick referring to his girl friend. And Crashaw would relegate the Lucastas and Antheas of contemporary literature, once for all, to the realm of the imaginary. I take for genuine the sentiment of his epigram on marriage:

I would be married, but I'd have no wife—
I would be married to a single life.

After all, there is not much point in it if it simply means that, as the Fellow of a college, Crashaw had a preference for remaining a bachelor. "Married" surely means "vowed" to a single life; the amorous feelings which Herrick distributed among so many putative milk-maids should, for Crashaw, be sublimated into the love of God. It is conceivable that the Mrs. M. R. to whom the prayer-book was sent was something more than a mere acquaintance. It was an age of spiritual affinities; the seventeenth century was inspired, at its opening, by the holy association between St. Francis of Sales and St. Jane Frances of Chantal, was disenchanted of that ideal, only at its close, by the antics of Madame Guyon and Père Lacombe. But there is no valid reason why we should suspect, in Crashaw, even that amount of condescension to human weakness. The she-saints of Christendom were his romance; most noticeably St. Mary Magdalen, a common devotion in the seventeenth century, and St. Theresa of Avila, only just canonized, appealing to her age much as her namesake of Lisieux appeals to our own.

You will see what I am getting at. If Crashaw wrote little, if what he wrote was but little castigated, it was because he was, first and foremost, an ascetic, unmoved by the thought of literary fame. The anonymous editor of 1646 describes him as "leading his life in St. Mary's church near St. Peter's College . . . where, like a primitive saint, he offered more prayers in the night than others usually offer in the day". Father Miles Pinkney, who edited, in 1652, the collection of his works called *Carmen Deo Nostro*, tells us how Crashaw "was beloved by all, dispraised by none . . . nor would he give nor take offence, befall what might; he would possess himself . . . forestalled with heavenly riches, which had wholly called his

thoughts from earth . . . What he might eat or wear he took
no thought; his needful food he rather found than sought" and
so on; the whole preface is not an appreciation, it is a hagiography. And Cowley, as we know, did not shrink from using
the word "saint" in recalling his memory:

> Poet and saint! To thee alone are given
> The two most sacred names of earth and heaven;
> The hard and rarest union which can be
> Next that of Godhead with Humanity . . .

(I think Cowley is right there and Bremond wrong.) And
lower down:

> His faith, perhaps, in some nice tenets might
> Be wrong; his life, I'm sure, was in the right;
> And I myself a Catholic will be
> So far at least, great saint, to pray to thee!

Even making allowances for the encomiastic fashion of the day,
these are no ordinary tributes. To the people who really knew
him, Crashaw was not just a pious sort of poet. He was a holy
man who wrote verses.

So much is a plain matter of history; the further suggestion
I want to make is a matter of guesswork. I believe the real
fact about Crashaw is that he was a mystic. Not in the sense
of a man who writes esoteric poetry, as Vaughan did, and
Traherne. A mystic, as such, does not write poetry; he has
better things to do. He is a man whose prayer aspires to get
rid not of words merely, but of thoughts; to pass, even,
beyond any conscious acts of the will, and to repose in God
by some other faculty for which we have no name, that touches
somehow, and more immediately, the divine.

It was the atmosphere of contemporary France. In Spain,
the great age of mysticism was the sixteenth century, the
period of St. Theresa and St. John of the Cross. In France, it

begins with St. Francis of Sales and the fathers of the French
Oratory; it flourishes in a hundred different coteries, whose
history has been preserved to us in the great work of Abbé
Bremond; with the condemnation of the *Maximes des Saints* in
1699 it suffers eclipse. That this movement had repercussions
in England is certain; indeed, to some extent the writings of
an English refugee, Father Benet Canfield, seem to have been
responsible for inaugurating it. If Crashaw caught the infection,
it is not likely to have been from his fellow-Anglicans, even at
Little Gidding. But books were at his disposal; and it was
natural that such an admirer of St. Theresa should indoctrinate
himself, somehow, with the tenets of mysticism.

> O thou undaunted daughter of desires
> By all thy dower of lights and fires,
> By all the eagle in thee, all the dove,
> By all thy lives and deaths of love,
> By thy large draughts of intellectual day,
> And by thy thirsts of love more large than they . . .
> By all of him we have in thee
> Leave nothing of myself in me;
> Let me so read thy life, that I
> Unto all life of mine may die.

It was not probable that her poet would let the matter rest
there, would be content with a mere literary appreciation of
the thing she stood for.

In the dedication of the prayer-book to Mrs. M. R. he
manifests the same attraction, referring to

> . . . that sacred store
> Of hidden sweets and holy joys,
> Words which are not heard with ears
> (Those tumultuous shops of noise),
> Effectual whispers, whose still voice
> The soul itself more feels than hears;

> Amorous languishments, luminous trances,
> Sights which are not seen with eyes . . .
> Delicious deaths, soft exhalations
> Of soul, dear and divine annihilations . . .
> And many a mystic thing
> Which the divine embraces
> Of the dear spouse of spirits with them will bring,
> For which it is no shame
> That dull mortality must not know a name.

Something you have there which George Herbert never wrote about. But it is in the Epiphany hymn that you get the clearest picture of Crashaw as a mystic; he refers by name to the Pseudo-Dionysius, a fifth-century author from whom the whole mystical tradition of the Church seems to derive; he alludes explicitly to that darkness, that suspension of the senses and the soul's faculties, which is the very condition of the divine union. The "right-eyed Areopagite" is represented as deriving his inspiration from the darkness of the stable at Bethlehem:

> Thus shall that reverend child of light,
> By being first scholar of this new night,
> Come forth great master of the mystic day,
> And teach obscure mankind a more close way
> (By the frugal, negative light
> Of a most wise and well-abuséd night)
> To read more legible thine original ray
> And make our darkness serve thy day.

Had Crashaw handled, or did he only know by quotation, that strange medieval treatise, *The Cloud of Unknowing*, so faithful to the doctrine of the Pseudo-Denys, so influential in forming the whole tradition of later mysticism?

Mystics do not write while they are praying—except Madame Guyon, who, I am afraid, was bogus. The reason is obvious; you can only write with images in your mind, and of such images your mystic, if he would pray, is the iconoclast. I would not, then, suggest that it made any difference to Crashaw's writing, what kind of prayer he used. But I think, if he was in the mystical tradition, it would explain one thing about his writing, his great want of self-criticism. To reflect, to turn back upon yourself, is the enemy of contemplation; it is to cloud the view of God with your own shadow. I see Crashaw, then, coming back from his prayer to his poetry with a great wealth of images running through his brain—all the more tumultuously, perhaps, for their recent cold-shouldering. He plays round his theme untiringly, seeing it from a hundred angles, and each view must go down on paper. He is writing for St. Mary Magdalen, for St. Theresa, not for a set of critics who will read it over his shoulder and say, "This is good . . . that is bad." So you get the glorious second stanza of "The Weeper":

> Heavens thy fair eyes be,
> Heavens of ever-falling stars;
> 'Tis seed-time still with thee,
> And stars thou sowest, whose harvest dares
> Promise the earth to countershine
> Whatever makes heaven's forehead fine.

And lower down:

> Not in the evening's eyes
> When they red with weeping are
> For the sun that dies,
> Sits sorrow with a face so fair;
> Nowhere but here did ever meet
> Sweetness so sad, sadness so sweet.

Then, before you know where you are:

> And now where he strays
> Among the Galilean mountains,

Or more unwelcome ways
He's followed by two faithful fountains;
Two walking baths, two weeping motions,
Portable, and compendious oceans.

Well, George Herbert can fall pretty flat; he it was that
wrote: "What can be lower than the common manger?" But
there is no thud, because he falls from no great height. How
could Crashaw, we ask, so forget himself? But you see, he was
forgetting himself. He wasn't thinking about Richard Crashaw, he was thinking about Mary Magdalene.

How inexhaustible his fancy is! Some of his best work was
done in the form of translation; and yet they are not really
translations, *Dies Irae*, *Stabat Mater*, *Vexilla Regis*, *Lauda Sion*,
Adoro te Devote—they are all a kind of midrash; it is what
Crashaw would have written, if Crashaw had been the author
of the original. You get an excellent example of that in the
lines:

Credo quidquid dixit Dei Filius;
Nil hoc verbo veritatis verius.

We have a translation of the *Adoro te* from the hand of a
modern poet who has much in common with Crashaw, Gerard
Manley Hopkins. And I do not know that you could better
his rendering:

What God's Son hath told me, take for truth I do;
Truth itself speaks truly, or there's nothing true

—perfect English idiom, and yet it contains just what was in the
original. Now watch Crashaw tackling the same couplet:

Faith is my force, faith strength affords
To keep pace with those powerful words;
And words more sure, more sweet than they,
Love could not think, truth could not say—

Excellent, but he could not be content to give a rendering of St. Thomas, he must bring St. Bonaventure in too. The words must be sweet as well as true; if it is truth that says them, it must nevertheless be love that thinks them. You cannot circumscribe such genius.

I have been writing about a Cambridge man who, if Antony à Wood's rather fishy story is to be trusted, went to Oxford before he went abroad, and became an Oxford man—and I have never rubbed it in. A man, too, who began life as a member of the Church of England, and became, instead, a member of the Church of Rome—and I have forgotten to rub that in either. I have only been concerned to interpret such a man as would have adorned, by his genius, any university, and, by his holiness, any Church; and I would rather stand worshipping at his shrine than make it a text for controversy.

PASCAL

THERE will always be room for more books about Pascal. And they will always be written; the French have a genius for reinterpretation, they prefer to reinterpret their fellow countrymen, and among those—even among those—Pascal takes indisputably high rank. In some ways, he has a rarity which one is tempted to write down as uniqueness. If there is such a thing—how *he* would have hated the phrase! —as "religious genius", Pascal, evidently, must be so described. And what other "religious genius" in all history is there whose name would have been written among the Immortals even if he had never written a word, never entertained a thought, on the subject of religion? Here is a mathematician, a scientist, of world consequence, to whom, in his innermost thoughts, science and mathematics were dross.

Again, what other recipient of a mystical experience has served it up for posterity (if the expression may be allowed) hot from the oven? Père Poulain tells us of a philosopher who thought to read the riddle of existence by putting himself under the influence of a certain drug, leaving paper and pencil handy so that he could write down the great secret just before the fumes overpowered him. When he came to, and staggered back to the table in search of the revelation, he found that he had written down the words "A strong smell of turpentine prevails throughout". That is the crux of the matter—how to be sure that our impressions of the irrecoverable moment have not been falsified by reflection? The revelations made to St. Gertrude, John Wesley's memories of his conversion—

they were written down afterwards; they are emotion remembered in tranquillity. But the Memorial, that scrap of paper which Pascal wore round his neck in memory of 23rd November 1654, bears all the marks of being fresh from the mint. He wrote when the experience was over, since he can tell us how long it lasted, from half-past ten till about half an hour after midnight. But the loosely connected texts, the fragmentary aspirations, are seen to spring from the unconscious mind, in which all inspiration, true or false, must needs be focused. The variations in the size of the handwriting (Bremond gives you the document in facsimile) tell the same story. Rigidly an experimentalist, Pascal could not even pass through the crisis of his soul without wanting to get it down, at the first possible moment, on paper.

But it is not only his rare qualities that make him a subject for perpetual reinterpretation; it is also the elusiveness of his personality. We are for ever trying to see the man behind the message, and it is a baffling exercise because we are not quite sure that we have fixed the attitude of his mind exactly right. Here there is a tempting parallel in the case of Newman. There is much in common between the two men: the admirably limpid style which makes it all too easy for the reader— and perhaps for the writer—to be carried away by the argument; the want of sympathy for scholastic methods; the destiny which allotted to either dangerous comrades-in-arms, with whom he was not altogether in sympathy. But especially there is this quality of elusiveness; what did Pascal, what did Newman feel *behind* it all? Critics have not been wanting who claimed that either man was, at the roots of him, an atheist.

And yet, what a vast difference in our apparatus for getting a personal impression of the two men! Newman so intimately self-revealed, so jealously scrutinized by friend and foe, who have left their impressions on record—and yet nobody, least of all himself, has really made it clear what happened to New-man's outlook between 1828 and 1830. How, then, are we to get any glimpse into the inner thoughts of Pascal, so anonymous in his influence, so much a figure behind the scenes, alternately whitewashed by Jansenist and by orthodox admirers? Port-Royal had a regular vice for hagiography; all geese were swans, and Pascal must be written up as something next door to a saint. If you would know anything about a man's *naturel*, you do not go to the annalists of Port-Royal for it; they disapproved, *ex hypothesi*, of the *naturel*. Only a stray allusion in a letter from his sister allows us to guess that Pascal had an atrabilious temperament, kept under control with difficulty; and yet how can your judgments on a man be valid if a fact like that is left out of sight?

The Pascal of the Memorial, and the Pascal of the *Provincial Letters*—how are we to bridge the gap between them? Fourteen months have elapsed, and a John Wesley suddenly reappears as a Jonathan Swift. If you take them in detail, the criticisms levelled at the *Provincial Letters* can be disposed of. You may say that the extracts chosen from the casuists, though not representative, were nevertheless characteristic. You may say that the volte-face by which the Thomist view of grace, at first ridiculed, is later on pressed into the service of Jansenism was due to a change in Nicole's attitude, not in Pascal's. You may say that Port-Royal was forced into a polemical frame of mind by the determined attacks made on it, and Pascal with the rest—even in his Memorial he will have it that God is not the God of the philosophers or the *savants*. You may defend his statement that he did not belong to Port-Royal on the ground that he did not belong to any Jansenist organization (but did Arnauld? Did Nicole?). You may think that Mère Angélique and M. Singlin were only shocked by the *Letters* because they terribly lacked a sense of humour. But you cannot get over the impression that a false note has been

struck. A man of first-class mind, newly converted to a
religion of desperate seriousness, has brought theology down
to the level of the man in the street; has taken up a weapon
of raillery which will be fatally borrowed by Voltaire.

There is fresh ground for speculation about Pascal's later
years, not least about the conflict between his Catholic and
his Jansenist loyalties. Did he really help to draft the *Mande-
ment*; did he lend himself to that compromise by which the
religious of Port-Royal were to disown Jansen's condemned
propositions without committing themselves to the assertion
that these propositions were to be found in Jansen's writings?
That compromise broke the heart of Jacqueline, his own
sister; was his conscience so much less tender than hers?
Later, it was notoriously Pascal who held out for a more
intransigent policy, when Nicole and Arnauld were for con-
ciliation. To be sure, there was no logical inconsistency in
that; but it looks as if there had been a psychological development at which we can only guess. Thenceforward, Pascal and
the Port-Royalists drew apart; was it, as some hold, because
he thought they had been too complaisant? Or did he, as
others think, draw back from his Jansenist position? Or did
he draw back from his Jansenist position on the ground that
the cause was not worth fighting for at all unless you were
prepared to fight for it *à outrance*? These questions were not
solved on his deathbed, because the priest who attended him,
Père Beurrier, first gave an edifying account of his Catholic
dispositions, then retracted, then retracted his retractation.
The biographers are left to wrangle.

Meanwhile, Pascal had bequeathed to the world a whole
collection of disjointed fragments, some of which—but how
many of them? Nobody is quite sure—were to be incorporated
in his projected apology for the Christian religion. That it
would have been a masterpiece of literature there can be no
doubt; if Pascal had never written anything else, he would still

be remembered by his fragments. But would it have been a convincing apology? Quite certainly, it would not have followed the traditional lines of theodicy. Pascal distrusted *a priori* arguments; had he not shown that the vacuum existed, when Père Noël had proved that it could not? And he would solve a more momentous question, whether that Plenum exists without which all our human life would be a vacuum, on other lines than the scholastic thinkers who had gone before him. He would appeal to facts; to the facts of human nature, in its heights and in its depths, to the facts of Jewish history, to the facts of the Incarnation. What appeal would such an apology have for our own day? Would it have satisfied the modern mind by its revolt from metaphysics? Or would it have antagonized the modern mind by its reliance on a fundamentalist view of Scripture? All this can be argued and re-argued, as we fit together, now this way, now that, the dazzling fragments of that tessellated pavement which Pascal never lived to finish.

And behind it all lies the doubt whether he was attempting the impossible, or whether he was solving at a blow the age-long difficulty of apologetics, when he set out to convince man's mind and man's heart at a single stroke, instead of appealing first to the one and then to the other. Would the finished work have been a rival to the *Summa Contra Gentes*, or a rival to the *Exercises*? Or would it, miraculously, have been a rival to both? Posthumously, as in life and in death, Pascal remains an enigma; there can be no certainty how the work would have grown in such hands as his. All he has left us is the ruins of a temple which was never built.

DR. JOHNSON

GRATITUDE, Dr. Johnson said, is a fruit of great culti-vation; you do not find it among gross people. The same is surely true of wit, as that term has any mean-ing for literature. Wit demands a soil of civilisation to grow in; it will not spring up self-sown, like the ale-house humour of a Villon. Commonly, too, wit will derive its colour and character from its own environment; and what one generation takes for granted as part of its standpoint, the next generation may see as something absurd, satirizable—our great-grand-fathers are a joke to us for having made a joke out of Brown, Jones, and Robinson. With this shifting of humour-values, how is it that any residuum defies the centuries? Perhaps because there is a subtle quality about the really great wits which is not of the period to which they belong. Not in the sense that they are misfits, that they are unrepresentative of their periods; Johnson could only have happened in the middle of the eighteenth century, and it is difficult enough to believe that he happened then. Rather in the sense that they over-flow the common water-courses, and leave a saline deposit for after ages to admire.

It would be out of place to give biographical details here about one who, whatever else he was, must certainly be regarded as the prince of biographees. Enough to say that he was born in the year of Malplaquet, and lived to see the loss of the American colonies. He missed John Evelyn by two years, Pepys by four; he died in the birth-year of Leigh Hunt. The eighteenth century may be pictured as a rather sluggish estuary, through which the stream of English history debouches upon the ocean of its modern achievement. Johnson bestrides it like a colossus.

To call Johnson a wit is a curiously inadequate definition of him. If anyone should study his life with the idea of cultivating the art of repartee, the effect would be disastrous. Tell us if you will, with Cibber, that Johnson knocked you down with the butt of his pistol if it failed to go off, or tell us with Garrick that "Johnson gives you a forcible hug, and shakes the laughter out of you whether you will or no"; the plain fact is that his idea of scoring a personal triumph in conversation hardly ever rose above the private school level. When he is asked, importunately, why he went to Mrs. Abington's benefit performance, where he could neither see nor hear, he is content to reply, "Because, Sir, she is a favourite of the public, and when the public cares the thousandth part for you that it does for her, I will go to your benefit too." When somebody defends Dominicetti's vapour baths: "Well, Sir, go to Dominicetti, and get thyself fumigated, but be sure that the stream be directed to thy head, for that is the peccant part." And when it is agreed that, for his own sake, a spend-thrift must be induced to leave London as soon as may be, Boswell is (quite gratuitously) attacked: "Nay, Sir, we'll send you to him. If that does not drive a man out of his house, nothing will." Was Johnson subjected to attacks of liver? More probably, I think—you cannot be certain, once the tones of a man's voice are silenced in death—he was one of those boisterous people who have no conception how much confusion their ill manners occasionally heap on the sensitive. But whatever the cause, it is certain that Johnson hardly ever scored a real success with a purely personal repartee. He never made Boswell look a fool *qua* Boswell, only *qua* Scot. His genius was for generalisation, not for satirizing the individual.

Was Johnson, then, a wit in the sense of producing readily

in conversation those flashy pieces of comment upon life which used to go by the name of epigrams, but in these last few years have been very regrettably labelled "wisecracks"? My impression is that Johnson could, because almost anybody could, but that he seldom did, because he realised almost anybody could. Take a phrase like the one he uses about Law, author of the *Serious Call*, and his admiration for Jacob Behmen, "whom Law alleged to have been somewhat in the same state with St. Paul, and to have seen unutterable things. Were it even so, said Johnson, Jacob would have resembled St. Paul still more, by not attempting to utter them"—that is only smart talking, and a hundred people can do it for you in any generation. A gentleman who had been unhappy in marriage, married again immediately after his wife died; Johnson said it was the triumph of hope over experience—but quickly, you feel, for fear somebody else should say it first. "In lapidary inscriptions a man is not upon oath", "I never take a nap after dinner, but when I have had a bad night, and then the nap takes me", "There is less flogging in our great schools than formerly, but then less is learned there, so that what the boys get at one end they lose at the other"—all this is well enough, but it is curiously not characteristic Johnson. Or, to speak more accurately, it is not characteristic Boswell-Johnson. All these last five quotations were "communicated" to Boswell by friends, not heard and reported by him. It is to be remembered, always, that we see Johnson refracted through a glass hardly less peculiar than himself; he may have made a lot of witty remarks, in the current fashion, which have not been preserved to us because Boswell did not happen to think them interesting. Literature is so overstocked with witty remarks in the current fashion; perhaps it is a good thing that Boswell, by accident or design, did leave that region unexplored, and concentrated on the more proper fruits of his friend's genius, the unquestionable Johnsoniana.

What is the nature of these; what is it that gives them their wholly individual flavour? Why are we quite certain that we should not dare to recommend Gibbon or Horace Walpole to a friend who wanted to read something "like" the life of Johnson? I despair of any attempt at accurate definition. What I mean to do here, is to indicate a few of the qualities in which Johnson's conversation excels, and to collect a few instances under each heading to illustrate the kind of excellence I mean. Probably my choice would not be everybody's choice; but if it suffices to illustrate, I am content.

In the first place, the Johnsonian dictum is apt to take your breath away by its sudden penetration of thought. You may think the sentiment wholly untrue, wholly misleading, and yet the fact remains that there was a way of looking at the facts which you had never thought of, although you had had the facts under review scores of times—and Johnson seemed to read his way straight into them. "In the House of Commons there are members enough who will not vote what is grossly unjust or absurd. No, Sir, there must always be right enough, or appearance of right, to keep wrong in countenance." "The rod produces an effect which terminates in itself . . . whereas, by exciting emulation, and comparisons of superiority, you lay the foundation of lasting mischief." "Every man has a right to utter what he thinks truth, and every other man has a right to knock him down for it. Martyrdom is the test." Democratic government—corporal punishment—religious toleration—you would have thought it impossible to rough out, and on the spur of the moment, three such unhackneyed methods of approach to three such hackneyed subjects of debate. Johnson's temptation was, no doubt, to say the unpopular thing, as it was certainly his temptation in argument to take, merely for that reason, the unpopular side. But it is to be remembered that he was in revolt against cant, living in an age of dawning sentimentalism. "When a butcher tells you that his heart bleeds for his country he has, in fact, no uneasy feeling." He was in revolt against the noble savage. "Do not allow yourself, Sir, to be imposed upon by such gross absurdity; it is sad stuff, it is brutish. If a bull could speak, he might as well say, Here am I with this cow and this grass, what being can enjoy greater felicity?" And he was in revolt, by anticipation, against the modern anthropology that has superseded Rousseau: "What account of their religion can you suppose to be learnt from savages? Only consider, Sir, our own state . . . ask the first ten gross men you meet, and hear what they can tell you of their religion."

I must not, however, be thought to suggest that Johnson is by preference and by trade a paradox-monger. Considering how steadily Boswell plied the arts of the "interviewer", and how commonplace on the whole Boswell's views were, it does credit to his friend that he was not driven more frequently into eccentricities of opinion. But Johnson did not need controversy to knock out sparks from the tinder-box of his prompt mind. "People are influenced by what a man says, if his practice is suitable to it—because they are blockheads. I have all my life long been lying till noon, yet I tell all young men, and tell them with great sincerity, that nobody who does not rise early will do any good." Johnson did not merely say that; he thought it. "Music is a method of employing the mind, without the labour of thinking at all, and with some applause from a man's self." Quite unmusical himself, Johnson could look over the player's shoulder, and detect the glance of self-admiration. Less cynically, "Every man thinks meanly of himself for not having been a soldier, or not having been at sea"; we shall find the generosity of the sentiment more striking when we reflect that England, as late as the Napoleonic wars, used, and was content to use, the press-gangs as its machinery of recruitment. Johnson was prepared to "debunk" false sentiment when he found it, but I do not think he had any instinct of cynicism. "Hell is paved with good intentions"—yes, but that means with good resolutions which were never kept, not with misguided efforts at philanthropy, if you consult the original context.

Sometimes it is not the thought itself, but a twist given to the expression of the thought, which takes your breath away. Especially, as became the author of a dictionary, Johnson was meticulous about the exact details of an expression. He would correct you, perhaps, frivolously, when you had been over-enthusiastic; the Giant's Causeway was worth seeing, yes, but not worth going to see; no, he had not come back highly gratified from Mrs. Montagu's evening entertainment, "yet I do not recollect to have passed many evenings with fewer objections". And if, in these minor encounters of life, he reminds us too much of Professor Crookshank at Mrs. Mount-stuart-Jenkinson's dinner-party—"He pores over an inaccuracy of expression like a domestic hen"—we are constantly made to realize the value of the instinct where graver issues are concerned. When somebody doubts, for example, whether the whole of Sennacherib's army, all those thousands, can really have been destroyed: "You are not to suppose that the angel of the Lord went about and stabbed each of them with a dagger, or knocked them on the head, man by man." And again, when Miss Seward maintains that annihilation would not, after all, be such a very dreadful thing: "The lady confounds annihilation, which is nothing, with our apprehension of it, which is dreadful." Nobody, when he liked, had better powers of showing you where you were wrong, how your tackling of the question was faulty, than Johnson had.

But the intellectual trick which is perhaps most characteristic of him is that of coining a phrase, usually with one good long word at the heart of it, to act as ballast, which sets on record for all time, marmoreally, Johnson's attitude to this or that, this person or that. It is probably a mistake to think of Johnson as specially fond of long words; certainly a mistake to think you can parody Johnson by using a lot of long words. He wrote at a period when long words were used; what is probably the best sentence in his *Journey to the Western Islands* is written, I think, entirely in monosyllables. But he had a playful love of using a long word now and again for its judicial effect; it was a kind of signature. Thus, when Boswell returned from abroad, and boasted of the indiscriminate lion-hunting which had taken him to see Rousseau, there was a sudden drop in the atmosphere; good heavens, was Rousseau a bad man? Well, in a way, perhaps, but you wouldn't think of him as a bad man in the same sense as Voltaire? "Why, Sir, it is difficult to settle the proportion of iniquity between them." The long word is not quite essential; it is enough that a word should be sent spinning into circulation with a fresh shade of meaning to it. "Yes, Burke *is* an extraordinary man; his stream of mind is perpetual"—Boswell once tried to quote that, for he was fond of quoting Johnson to himself without acknowledgment, and it came out as "Burke has a constant stream of conversation." But in general the long word is preferred; "he might have ripened into an atheist" would do, but "he might have exuberated into an atheist" is the perfect form of the sentiment. So, we often say that it would be easy to do a thing if you gave up your mind to it; what a subtle sting was added to that formula when Johnson declared of "Ossian" that "a man might write such stuff for ever, if he would abandon his mind to it"!

Sometimes the effect of the polysyllable is to recall us to a judicial standpoint. *The Beggar's Opera*, like the crook-film of to-day, was often accused of indoctrinating minds with the first notions of crime. Johnson expressed himself doubtful about this; but then, as if feeling a condemnation would be expected from him, added, "There is in it such a labefactation of all principles, as may be injurious to morality.'' Sometimes it does justice to the mysterious character of the subject-matter under discussion. We, with the smattering of psycho-logical jargon we have picked up from books which know nothing about it, how ready we are to dismiss what puzzles us with chips of inadequate metaphor! Which of us does not talk gaily of ''kinks'' in his mental make-up; as if it were an ascertained fact that our mental make-up is a long, straight piece of wire, which can only show any variableness or shadow of turning when somebody has been tying knots in it without our knowledge? How much more adequately, because much less positively, will Johnson write of our odd tricks of thought: ''Among the anfractuosities of the human mind, I know not if it may be one, that there is a superstitious reluctance to sit for a picture.'' The human mind, you see, is conceived as a deep bay, full of inlets and caverns; how just an estimate! Sometimes the long words will paint a picture more alluringly than their short synonyms could; witness the rousing and wholly justified comment when Thrale's brewery was sold: ''We are not here to sell a parcel of boilers and vats, but the potentiality of growing rich beyond the dreams of avarice.'' And sometimes the long words express what it would have been impossible to express anyhow else. No sounder reason was ever produced by a guest for habitual lateness at breakfast, than when Johnson reminded Mrs. Thrale of the one occasion on which he came down too early: ''Madam, I do not like to come down to vacuity.'' The vacuity of a country house early in the morning, who does not know it? Except those fortunate people who are always, and by instinct, late for breakfast.

It must not be thought for a moment, I repeat, that Johnson used long words because he did not know how to express himself clearly, or because he did not know how to express himself vigorously, in any other way. Imagine any modern author writing about so dull a subject as the birth-rate of Russia.

Hundreds of them do; welcoming it, deploring it, terrified of it, distrustful of the statistics, and so on; but always in technical language, with a great deal about index figures and standards of living and expectation of tenure and God knows what. Curiously, the birth-rate of Russia was a subject which aroused interest in the England of Dr. Johnson's time; at least, it aroused interest in the capacious bosom of Dr. Johnson himself. And this is his comment on it: "It is not from reason and providence that people marry, but from inclination. A man is poor; he thinks, I cannot be worse, and so I'll e'en take Polly." If only our modern professors would teach us economics in such language, and with a similar regard for the concrete realities of life, one might begin to understand what the modern world is all about.

What probably won Johnson his chief fame as a conversationalist was his ready habit of providing illustration, on the spur of the moment, for the point he wanted to enforce. Occasionally it is all a little wooden; you get hints of a formula. Thus, "All power, of whatever sort, is of itself desirable. A man would not submit to learn to hem a ruffle of his wife or his wife's maid; but if a mere wish could attain it, he would rather wish to be able to hem a ruffle." Or again, "If a physician were to take to eating horseflesh, nobody would employ him, though one may eat horseflesh, and be a very skilful physician." I can conceive that on his off days there was a good deal of this sort of thing; and perhaps if Boswell had written down more of those conversations which he tearfully accuses himself of having left unrecorded, we should have been able to comprise one or two of these overworked gambits under algebraical symbols. But, even when the form of the argument is stereotyped, how rich is the fancy which supplies the illustrations! Why is it that when we are hunting about, in conversation, for an analogy which will illustrate our point, we never think of hemming ruffles or of eating horseflesh?

Here is a case where the whole phrase is imaginative: "There is not a sapling upon Parnassus more severely blown about by every wind of criticism than that poor fellow"; we are not told who the unfortunate author was, but what a picture we have of him! There is the same vigour of simile about Johnson's answer to the friend who extolled the generosity of the British sailor: "I do not call a tree generous, that sheds its fruit at every breeze." On a shy boy being sent to a public school—not a subject you would have expected to evoke his more discerning sympathy—he comments, "Placing him at a public school is forcing an owl upon day." In this connection, try as you will, you cannot avoid using one or two hackneyed examples. The *congé d'élire*, for instance—Johnson had only overheard it being discussed, and there was no need to say anything on the question raised, whether it was in truth a recommendation or an out-and-out command; what he did say was, "It is such a recommendation, as if I should throw you out of a two-pair-of-stairs window, and recommend you to fall soft." And of course there is the comment on the Quaker lady's preaching, "like a dog's walking on his hinder legs. It is not done well, but you are surprised to find it done at all." There is such a lot of wisdom gathered up in that phrase, and it applies to such a lot of other things besides ladies speaking in public—if it does apply to ladies speaking in public.

Why did Johnson decry the Scots? Was the antipathy a natural one; or did he cultivate it; and if so, did he cultivate it out of perversity, or as a kind of literary asset? After all, it is no bad thing for the reputation of a humorist if there is known to be one particular subject that will "set him off", one recurring joke in his writings which appears in a hundred forms, but always at the expense of the same institution. I think the quarrel with the Scots was real, though perhaps ill-defined. When it was suggested that he disliked them because they betrayed their king at the time of the Civil War, he claimed that it was a good enough reason, but did not identify it as his own. I fancy it was a temperamental want of sympathy —Lamb, it will be remembered, owns to it—exaggerated in Johnson's case by the feeling that the Scots were spreading all over the place and having everything their own way, in literature especially. It was the age of Hume, of Beattie, of Robertson, of Macpherson, of Reid, of Adam Smith. Individually, Johnson liked meeting these people, because he liked meeting nearly everybody who would consent to argue with him. But viewed as a whole, this southward movement across the border was an invasion of Presbyterianism and of Whiggery; "Hume, Sir, was a Tory only by chance." After as before his tour in the Hebrides, Johnson thought of the Scots as a real menace.

At the same time, the circumstance that Boswell has been the chief recorder of his conversation has no doubt exercised a profound influence on what Johnson said (as opposed to what he thought) about the Scots. What he said is probably a good deal less violent than what he thought; but it is also much cleverer, more subtly malicious. He obviously enjoyed pulling (I can find no more respectful phrase for it) Boswell's leg. This was a delicate business; for, if the humour was too broad, the honest Scottish laugh came too easily; if it was too subtle, there was the danger that Boswell would not see the joke at all. Sometimes he did not see the joke at all. They were talking, one day, of the respect shown to soldiers in France; Boswell was surprised that they should be so much respected where they were so numerous. "Nay, Sir," replied Johnson, "wherever a particular character or profession is high in the estimation of a people, those who are of it will be valued above other men. We value an Englishman highly in this country, and yet Englishmen are not rare in it." This was quite above Boswell's head; he records it dutifully, but without comment.

The jokes against Scotland—if our friends from beyond the

Border will let us stand handkerchief in mouth for a moment or two, how good they are, even at their unfairest! The country itself: "Seeing Scotland, Madam, is seeing the flower fade away to the naked stalk"; and when Johnson loses his oak staff on the Isle of Mull, "It is not to be expected that any man in Mull who had got it will part with it. Consider, Sir, the value of such a piece of timber here." Persecuted on his native heath, Boswell must equally be persecuted in London; he tells Johnson, sycophantically to be sure, that Fleet Street is in his mind more delightful than Tempe: "Ay, Sir," returns the unpropitiated deity, "but let it be compared with Mull!" And as for the people, their learning is "like bread in a besieged city; every man gets a little, but no man gets a full meal." In a rash moment, Boswell wondered whether it was not an exaggeration to describe the death of Garrick as eclipsing the gaiety of nations, in the plural. "Nations may be said", was the imperturbable reply, "if we allow the Scotch to be a nation, and to have gaiety, which they have not." But perhaps the most graphic allusion of all is when Johnson is contributing his reminiscences of Dr. John Campbell, compiler of the *Biographia Britannica*: "Campbell is a good man, a pious man. I am afraid he has not been in the inside of a church for many years, but he never passes a church without pulling off his hat, which shows that he has good principles. I used to go pretty often to Campbell's on a Sunday evening, till I began to consider that the shoals of Scotchmen who flocked about him might probably say, when anything of mine was well done, Ay, ay, he has learnt this of Cawmell."

Was Johnson brutal to his biographer? Most of us, I think, will be disposed to acquit him of any such charge. He was, it is to be remembered, a man of a difficult nervous constitution, never far off, I suppose, from that state which is most easily described as "wanting to scream" This will account for some

94

of his ferocities in argument; it will account also for some of his impatience under misplaced kindness. "He sometimes could not bear being teazed with questions. I was once present when a gentleman asked so many . . . that he at last grew enraged, and said, I will not be put to the question . . . The gentleman, who was a good deal out of countenance, said, Why, Sir, you are so good, that I venture to trouble you. JOHNSON: Sir, my being so good is no reason why you should be so ill." How often I have wished I dared to quote that! And then there was Chambers, who would hang round suggesting remedies when he was ill: "Prythee, don't teaze me. Stay till I am well, and then you shall tell me how to cure myself." We have all felt like that; and if Johnson felt it a little too keenly, at least he expressed it with admirable humour.

But with Boswell I think he was singularly gentle in his reprimands, considering what a nuisance Boswell could evidently be. When, for example, he offered to "explain" the whole of Allan Ramsay's "Gentle Shepherd" to Johnson, he surely deserved something more severe than the retort, "No, Sir, I won't learn it. You shall retain your superiority by my not knowing it." You must be on easy terms with a friend— and a Scottish friend—when you can say to him, "Boswell, lend me sixpence, not to be repaid." Boswell was importunate, and continually demanding, in his letters especially, expressions of Johnson's good-will. If he had to be taught a lesson, how was he to be taught it more charmingly than this? "My regard for you is greater almost than I have words to express, but I do not choose to be always repeating it; write it down in the first leaf of your pocket-book, and never doubt of it again." Occasionally, the cross-questioning became more than flesh and blood could bear. Breaking the silence of the seas among the farthest Hebrides, "I asked him if he had ever been accustomed to wear a night-cap. He said, No. I asked, if it was not best to wear one. JOHNSON: Sir, I had this custom by chance, and perhaps no man shall ever know whether it is best to sleep with or without a night-cap.''

Not that Johnson resented the intrusion of the frivolous, or even the fantastic, into conversation. When Boswell asked what he would do if he were shut up in a castle, and a new-born child with him, after admitting that he would not like his company, he entered gloriously into the spirit of the thing. He would make a shed on the roof, and take it there for fresh air; he would feed it, and wash it much, and with warm water to please it. Although he was a teetotaller during most of the period when Boswell knew him, he had his own philosophy of eating: ''For my part, I mind my belly very studiously and very carefully, for I look upon it, that he who does not mind his belly, will hardly mind anything else.'' And he said once, ''This was a good dinner enough, to be sure, but it was not a dinner to ask a man to.'' That claret is the liquor for boys, port for men, but he who aspires to be a hero must drink brandy, is a remark which attests, at least, an interest in the cellar, though some may doubt its orthodoxy. Johnson was a man who knew how to give tongue when he was enjoying himself. ''Life has not many better things than this,'' he said, as he drove in a fast post-chaise; and although, when Boswell quoted this remark, he objected that you were driving rapidly *from* something or *to* something, as if he were bothering about means and ends, he admitted, later, that if he had no duties and no reference to futurity he would spend his life driving briskly in a post-chaise with a pretty woman. As for London, his love of it does not need to be attested by quotation. ''Why, Sir, Fleet Street has an animated appearance, but I think the full tide of human existence is at Charing Cross.''

This occasional note of frivolousness—impishness, almost— suffices to mark out Johnson clearly enough from the high-brows, of his own age or another. Once, I think, the devil of laughter got the better of him; it was when he was with

Boswell and Chambers, two Scots lawyers. Let Boswell tell his own story. "He now laughed immoderately, without any reason that we could perceive, at our friend's making his will; called him the *testator*, and added, I dare say he thinks he has done a mighty thing; he won't stay till he gets home to his seat in the country, to produce this wonderful deed; he'll call up the landlord of the first inn on the road, and . . . will tell him that he should not delay making his will; and here, Sir, he will say, is my will, which I have just made, with the assistance of one of the ablest lawyers in the kingdom, and he will read it to him (laughing all the time). . . . I trust you have had more conscience than to make him say, *being of sound understanding*, ha, ha, ha! I hope he has left me a legacy. I'd have his will turned into verse, like a ballad." And so on. To meet this quite irresponsible levity in the year 1773 is to me, I confess, the most surprising thing in Boswell. I am not worried, as Boswell was worried, about what Johnson found to laugh at; I think it was the faces of his companions that kept him going. But that it should, as Boswell points out, have been the author of the *Rambler*. . . .

A man whose understanding had a range and a depth unexampled, certainly in his period; yet would focus the ray of his fancy to illuminate any subject, however insignificant, the history of night-caps, it would seem, alone excepted.

A NEGLECTED POET (JAMES GRAINGER)

WHETHER we have lost the art of writing good poetry is a matter we debate vainly; those coxcombs, our grandsons, will have the say in the matter. A more terrible doubt sometimes occurs to you if you have the library habit—the habit, I mean, not of *reading* old books, but of taking them down from their shelves, opening them, smelling them, taking in the scope of them, skimming ten pages, and putting them back. What if we have lost the art of writing bad poetry? To be sure, we have still our bad poets, who, in their eagerness to benefit mankind, publish (and not infrequently distribute their work) at their own charges: they write prose for us, or pure journalese, or school-boy ineptitudes, or naked sentimentalism: they cut it up into lengths—some even rhyme it. It is bad; but is it bad poetry? Is it poetry at all? Not for such, the Muse Cacohymnia expostulates, are her crowns: her orgiasts must achieve bathos, and true bathos demands a perfect craftsmanship in verse, no false rhymes, no missing cæsuras, that bad taste, bad sentiment, bad imagination may find its just and inevitable expression. Bad verse you may find anywhere; bad poetry is of its essence a *faux ménage*— verbal felicity married to mental imbecility; to fall ludicrously the author must fall from a height—just as a hat-hunt cannot be properly enjoyed unless a top-hat be the quarry.

The art, indeed, is not wholly dead. It was a recent pen that wrote:

> If you glance at history's pages
> In all lands and eras known,

> You will find the buried ages
> Far more wicked than our own.
> As you scan each word and letter
> You will realize it more—
> That the world to-day is better
> Than it ever was before.

There is bathos here; but our modern, niminy-piminy metres are never a true diving-board for bathos. For it we still have to look back to Robert Montgomery and the extracts of Martinus Scriblerus:

> Behold Dalhousie, the great God of War,
> Lieutenant-colonel to the Earl of Mar——

how shall we recapture *that* cormorant-plunge?

James Grainger, born at the very nadir of the bathetic movement—at that very Dunse in Berwickshire which may have given philosophy Duns Scotus, and the English language a new term of abuse—has earned in works of little compass an uncontested niche on the slopes of Catabathmon. His name was only known to his contemporaries because he won, without deserving either, the vitriolic hatred of Smollett and the good-natured patronage of Dr. Johnson. He served Apollo with the lyre and the lancet indifferently, and an accident of trade depression forced him, to the eternal gratitude of posterity, to take over a practice in the West Indies. He owed it to himself to attempt the heroic couplet: a few dozen lines at the end of his Ode to Solitude give us a regretful glimpse of what he might have done working in that medium:

> When smooth old Ocean, and each storm's asleep,
> Then ignorance may plough the watery deep:
> But when the demons of the tempest rave,
> Skill must conduct the vessel through the wave . . .

and, soon afterwards:

> ~~Intrepid virtue triumphs~~ over fate—
> The good can never be unfortunate:
> And be this maxim graven on thy mind,
> "The height of virtue is to serve mankind."

But an obvious preference for Milton, which is not ashamed to take the form of frequent unacknowledged quotations, beckoned him to the less precipitous crags of blank verse in the classical manner. It was in that metre he composed his masterpiece: *The Sugar-cane: A Poem in Four Books*.

The selection and grouping of the matter is bad Virgil. The style is bad Milton. Add to this, that the subject of his choice is a process incurably pedestrian, the result of which can only be sugar or (at the best) rum: that while the Mantuan reaps corn Grainger hoes yams, while the Mantuan treads grapes Grainger must peel bananas; that local colour demands the superseding of the ash and the pine by the coconut; that machinery, which Grainger is far too conscientious to leave undescribed, does the greater part of the manufacture; that the human labour involved is not that of jolly Apulian swains but that of negroes looted from the Gold Coast, whose presence has begun to need some explanation, even to the easy conscience of the eighteenth century. The situation cries for bathos, and gets it.

> Nor tremulates the cocoa's airiest arch——

Yes, it is very much like the Georgics, only not quite the same.

> Some of the skilful teach, and some deny
> That yams improve the soil——

Milton might have written it, if only they hadn't been yams. "One might as well have written The Parsley Bed, a Poem," said Dr. Johnson, wrong for once: it would not have been nearly as funny.

> On yonder hill, that fronts the rising sun,
> With plantains and bananas bosomed deep——

There is nothing to touch that in a parsley-bed.

Grainger, indeed, seems to feel that his subject is imposed on him rather than chosen:

> Where pastoral Dyer, where Pomona's bard,
> And Smart and Somervile in varying strains
> Their sylvan lore convey, O may I join
> This choral band, and from their precepts learn
> To deck my theme, which, though to song unknown,
> Is most momentous to my country's weal.

Inspired to prophecy, he foresees the agricultural depression, foresees that the future of his beloved country depends upon her imports, and determines that such imports shall have their *vates sacer*, even though the theme, as he admits, will need a certain amount of "decking". The trouble is that the theme (like those unhappy mortals so framed by Nature that they cannot dress but can only put on clothes) only becomes the more incongruous the more conscientiously it is decked. What more necessary than to provide hints for first aid in case of a wetting? And yet

> Unhappy he, who journeys then from home,
> No shade to screen him! His untimely fate
> His wife, his babes, his friends will soon deplore,
> Unless hot wines, dry clothes, and friction's aid
> His fleeting spirits stay——

falls, somehow, short of the heroic note. Again, it is inevitable that a visitor, especially a medical visitor, to the tropics should be interested in the local entomology. And no doubt these things have their place in the scheme of creation:

> Yet musical those little insects' hum,
> That hover round us, and to Reason's ear
> Deep moral truths convey.

But, in poetry, one does not want to press the point, as in the lines

> Mosquitoes, sand-flies seek the sheltered roof,
> And with fell rage the stranger-guest assail,
> Nor spare the sportive child; from their retreats
> Cockroaches crawl displeasingly abroad——

and so on. Plain-speaking goes even further when, in justice to his subject, the author is compelled to describe the symptoms of "the blast", a disease which is apt to infect the sugar-cane itself:

> Unseemly stains succeed, which, nearer viewed
> By microscopic arts, small eggs appear,
> Dire fraught with reptile life: alas! too soon
> They burst their filmy gaol, and crawl abroad,
> Bugs of uncommon shape.

Even where his subject is such that it might have been securely treated by a less adventurous hand, a fatal rhetorical instinct betrays the poet to his fall; and he rises heroically from one ditch only to trip in another. He thus describes, for example, the collecting of the sugar-canes:

> These with their green, their pliant branches bound,
> (For not a part *of this amazing plant*
> But serves some useful purpose) charge the young:
> Not Idleness declines this easy toil;

E'en Lameness from its leafy pallet crawls
To join the favoured gang. What of the cane
Remains (*and much the largest part remains*)
Cut into junks a yard in length . . . etc.

And when he turns his hand to machines, little wonder that
he loses his nerve.

The chymist knows, when all-pervading fire
Bids the metalline ore abruptly flow,
What dread explosions, and what dire effects
A few cold drops of water will produce——

Why did not Scriblerus live to read that last line? But whole
passages must needs creep on the lower level.

To this be nailed three polished iron plates,
Whereupon three steel capouces turn with ease
Of three long rollers, twice nine inches round,
With iron cas'd, and jagg'd with many a cog.
The central cylinder exceeds the rest
In portly size, thence aptly captain named.
To this be riveted the extended sweeps;
And harness to each sweep two seasoned mules:
They, pacing round, give motion to the whole.
Fast flows the liquor through the lead-lined spouts,
And, depurated by opposing wires,
In the receiver floats a limpid stream.

Oh admirable faith of the eighteenth century, which would fit
the classical key to every lock!

The labourer is worthy of his hire, and Grainger is not insensible to the hedonistic aspect of the industry he celebrates.

Tell me, what viands land or streams produce
The large, black, female, moulting crab excel?

and, with yet more of abandonment:

> ~~But say, ye boon companions, in what strains,~~
> What grateful strains shall I record the praise
> Of their best produce, heart-recruiting rum?

But, take him at his usual level, he is a moralist with more than
the share of moralism common to his period. The brother-
hood of Man is a subject which excites him to his highest
fervour, though not, it must be admitted, to his most lyrical
flights.

> Then let not man, for little selfish ends,
> (Britain, remember this important truth!)
> Presume the principle to counteract
> Of universal love:

and again:

> Be pious, be industrious, be humane:
> Whate'er their creed, God is the sire of Man,
> His image they: then dare not thou, my son,
> To bar the gates of mercy on mankind——

(*The Sugar-cane*, it may be observed, was published in 1764;
Gray had had the good fortune to write his *Elegy* thirteen years
earlier.) And if our author seems at times disposed to exclude
France from the commonwealth of nations, it is only because
the French illustrate so admirably those very defects of justice
against which he points his moral. Thus, in a description of
the depredations caused by monkeys:

> Destructive, on the upland sugar-groves
> The monkey nation preys; with gambols they
> Pour o'er the cane-grove . . .
> So when, of late, innumerous Gallic hosts,
> Fierce, wanton, cruel, did by stealth invade
> The peaceable American's domains,
> No sooner Albion's martial sons advanced,

> Than the gay dastards to their forests fled,
> And left their spoils and tomahawks behind.

A still more serious accusation impeaches their methods of commercial rivalry:

> False Gallia's sons, that hoe the ocean isles

(Grainger always uses "hoe" in imitation of Virgil's *arare*, instead of a weaker verb such as "cultivate" or "till")

> False Gallia's sons, that hoe the ocean isles,
> Mix with their sugar loads of worthless sand,
> Fraudful, their weight of sugar to increase.
> Far be such guile from Britain's honest swains!
> Such arts, awhile, the unwary may surprise
> And benefit the impostor, but, ere long,
> The skilful buyer will the fraud detect,
> And, with abhorrence, reprobate thy name.

It would be difficult to find a clearer *exposé*, whether of the motives that inspire the action or of the considerations that should deter us from it.

The question naturally suggests itself, How far do these creditable sentiments of Grainger's affect his attitude towards the slave trade? We know that our forefathers had a conveniently lax conscience on the point, and that George Whitefield owned slaves, but how will the heroic manner stand the strain of such an inconsistency? Grainger feels the difficulty, and tries manfully to meet it. There are, naturally, regrettable incidents:

> When first your Blacks are novel to the hoe,
> Study their humours; some, soft, soothing words,
> Some, presents, and some, menaces subdue;
> And some I've known, so stubborn is their kind,
> Whom blows, alas, could win alone to toil.

But, even here, there is a wise moderation to be exercised:

> Ye, whom the knowledge of a living God
> Should lead to virtue, are ye free from crimes?
> Ah, pity then these uninstructed swains,
> And still let Mercy soften the decrees
> Of rigid Justice, with her lenient hand——

Justice, you know. Even apart from Mercy, there are practical considerations to affect our decision.

> Howe'er insensate some may deem their slaves,
> Nor 'bove the bestial rank, far other thoughts
> The Muse, soft daughter of Humanity,
> Will ever entertain. The Ethiop knows,
> The Ethiop feels, when treated like a man;
> Nor grudges, should necessity compel,
> By day, by night to labour for his lord——

Yes, there is the question of the overtime. Are there even darker sides to the picture? Probably not:

> Are there (the Muse can scarce believe the tale),
> Are there, who lost to every feeling sense,
> To Reason, interest lost—

("interest" is good)

>   —their slaves desert,
> Maim'd by imprudence, or the hand of Heaven?
> The good man feeds his blind, his aged steed,
> And dares a mortal to his fellow man
> (For, spite of vanity, thy slaves are men)
> Deny protection? Muse, suppress the tale.

Grainger, it may be observed, had married a daughter of the local Governor. Muse, suppress the tale! It is possible that we have to recognise in him the father of propaganda.

With all this preoccupation about humanity and the rights

of the negro, it is perhaps a pity that Grainger should have left us elaborate directions, all in the classical manner but with absolute *sang-froid*, as to the various breeds of slave and their selection for purposes of commerce. It is all very well for Virgil to give us the points of a good bull or a good stallion, as he does in Georgic III, 50 sqq., but Grainger seems to carry imitation rather far when he proceeds to write:

> But, planter, from what coast soe'er they sail,
> Buy not the old—they ever sullen prove;
> With heart-felt anguish they lament their home;
> They will not, cannot work, they never learn
> Thy native language; they are prone to ails,
> And oft by suicide their being end.
> Must thou from Afric reinforce thy gang?
> Let health and youth their every sinew firm,
> Clear roll their ample eye, their tongue be red,
> Broad swell their chest, their shoulders wide expand,
> Not prominent their belly, clean and strong
> Their thighs and legs in just proportion rise.
> Such soon will brave the fervours of the clime,
> And, free from ails that kill thy native train,
> A useful servitude will long support.

As a doctor, our poet may well have been interested in native diseases, but there is an irrepressible commercialism about all his references to them.

> There are (the Muse hath oft abhorrent seen)
> Who swallow dirt (so the chlorotic fair
> Oft chalk prefer to the most poignant cates);
> Such, dropsy bloats, and to sure death consigns;

and again:

> One precept more it much imports to know—
> The blacks who drink the Quanza's lucid stream,

> Fed by ten thousand springs, are prone to bloat,
> Whether at home or in these ocean isles;

and again, in the same matter-of-fact style:

> The slaves from Minnah are of stubborn breed;
> But, when the bill or hammer they affect,
> They soon perfection reach. But fly with care
> The Moco nation; they themselves destroy.
> Worms lurk in all, yet pronest they to worms
> Who from Mundingo sail——

and so on. What a poet!

Not that Grainger was at all insensible to the general discomforts which attend the life of a slave. After all this catalogue of the diseases to which they are subject, he turns to address the negroes, and points out that their lot is on the whole far preferable to that of the Scottish miners—a passage which suggests thoughts.

The poet tells us that "as the face of the country was wholly different from that of Europe, so whatever hand copied its appearances, however rude, could not fail to enrich poetry with many new and picturesque images". He has not failed. The poem (it really exists, and all the above quotations are perfectly genuine) needs to be read in full, as you may find it in vol. 59 of "British Poets", published by Whittingham in 1822. It is all quite perfect, and all quite perfectly wrong. It is a wonderful production.

THE INGOLDSBY LEGENDS

I HAVE an uneasy suspicion that a man who is asked to talk about the *Ingoldsby Legends* is being treated as a link with the past. Not indeed that I was alive a hundred years ago, when the Revd. R. H. Barham died. But I read the poems in my school-room days, without being conscious of doing anything old-fashioned. And how shall I recommend them to people who did not read them in the school-room? They belong to that class of literature (the novels of Surtees are another example) which you must read young if you are to re-read them with any pleasure in later life. They must come to you lavender-scented with the unconscious associations of childhood. Do not go away and say I encouraged you to read the *Ingoldsby Legends*, if you are too young to be dated by having read them when you were young.

I do not know that the biography of the author is very important to the understanding of what he wrote; but a thumbnail sketch, at least, is demanded by the occasion. He was born in the year 1788, preserving a due centenary distance from his present biographer. The son of an old family of small Kentish squires, he entered, as of right, into a patrimony of old legends and countryside superstitions which he was to place, later on, at the service of his Muse. He was educated at St. Paul's school, which developed in him, as in Chesterton, a certain literary precocity; his first volume of poems was published when he was nineteen. Perhaps even more importantly, he became the life-long friend of Bentley, the publisher; a friendship that brought with it an irritating stimulus to authorship. He matriculated at Brasenose College, Oxford, and seems to have entered into the spirit of that institution; it was he who explained to the Dean that "morning chapel at seven was really too late for him; unless he could get to bed by four or five he was really fit for nothing next day". Actually, he seems to have been one of those enviable people who, when they have put their friends to bed, can spend the rest of the night working.

In 1813 he took orders, two years ahead of Keble. He served his apprenticeship in a Kentish parish where smuggling was still a nightly event; then (in 1821) became a minor canon of St. Paul's, and afterwards priest in ordinary to the chapels royal. He was the friend of Theodore Hook and of Sydney Smith; but it was not till 1837 that he really embraced the literary career, to oblige a young man called Dickens, editor of *Bentley's Miscellany*. Between that year and 1845 he tossed off the three or four hundred pages of small print which are entitled *The Ingoldsby Legends*.

Whatever else you make of him, his facility was extraordinary. Some credit has been claimed for him as the reviver (with Byron) of an art extinct since *Hudibras*—that of inventing apparently impossible two-syllable and three-syllable rhymes. I mean such rhymes as: "A metaphor taken—I have not the page aright—Out of an ethical work by the Stagyrite" (which was apparently how he pronounced the birth-place of Aristotle); or "Till I've done—from my past scenes of folly a far actor—Some feat shall redeem both my wardrobe and character". Listeners with delicate ears will have gathered that there is a certain roughness about his methods. Yet I think he may fairly be claimed as the precursor, not only of those effects in Browning which scandalize so many of his readers, but of a tradition in humorous verse which reaches on through W. S. Gilbert to A. D. Godley, and is not yet extinct. Those who have made experiments of their own in this direction are sadly conscious that the trick is much easier to do than it appears from outside. You produce the far-fetched, the composite, the improbable rhyme *first*, and when its more reputable fellow appears at a suitable interval, the reader's ear is tickled by the occurrence of something inevitable; perhaps you can even flatter his vanity with the knowledge that he was expecting it.

What has more endeared Barham to his readers, I suspect, is his indomitable use of the dactylic rhythm, the accent of the line falling on every third syllable, instead of falling on every second. When you hear people of rather more than my age breaking out into senile guffaws over the well-known lines, "She took prussic acid without any water, And died like a Duke and a Duchess's daughter", you moderns will find it difficult to sympathize. But I think what unconsciously delights the old gentleman is the lilt of the thing; and it delights him, as I tried to explain just now, because it delighted him when he was a *young* gentleman. There is something congenial to boyhood about those tripping, dancing rhythms. Unashamedly, we liked their rollicking effect; you might keep your Shakespeare and your Tennyson—we wanted the *Bab Ballads* and Kipling. It wasn't very good taste, but it was honest.

Still, these are but tricks of the trade. Poetry wasn't all rhyme and scansion, even in the days when poetry rhymed and scanned. Barham's real gift, I fancy, was the raciness with which he could tell a story in verse, a kind of natural fluency which reminds you of the *Odyssey*. And he contrived to be— well, I will not say funny all the time, but jocular all the time. Not that we, who read the *Legends* in the school-room, bothered much about the jokes; they were largely topical, and meant nothing to us; it is the tragedy of the topical humorist that he dates so quickly. But there was a grimness about some of the legends which impressed us, I think, even more. Open at the very first poem, and you will come across the kind of thing I mean; it is called "The Hand of Glory", and the refrain runs: "Open lock, To the dead man's knock, Fly bolt, and bar, and band! Nor move, nor swerve, Joint, muscle, or nerve, At the spell of the dead man's hand! Sleep all who sleep, wake all who wake, But be as the dead for the dead man's sake!" That wasn't the kind of thing that made the business of going to bed any easier.

I think we were fond, too, without knowing it, of Barham's medievalism. His humour dates him; it is the humour of his period, the kind which indulges (for example) in elaborate euphemisms, to avoid mentioning unmentionable words like "hell" or "trousers". But he is not less dated by his subject-matter; he belongs to the Romantic Revival. Not all the pieces are medieval, but all the most popular, all the most character-istic. And the medieval ones were full of devils and mitred abbots and bare-footed friars and witches and bad barons and palmers and damsels; which meant a great deal in a book pub-lished (as Dickens was published) with illustrations almost more important than the text. What illustrations the *Ingoldsby Legends* had! True, the author was being funny about the Middle Ages, like the Ballad of Lord Bateman. But we got our devils and palmers all the same.

I can imagine my own co-religionists—among whom, by an odd freak of fate, some of Barham's own lineal heirs are numbered—being rather shocked upon opening the *Legends* for the first time. Not merely by their strange liturgical in-accuracy (the abbot who puts on a dalmatic and maniple to sit down to dinner), nor even by their loose interpretation of history (though Barham disbelieved in the story of the walled-up nun, which took in Sir Walter Scott). No, rather the general air of treating the old religion as something which no longer exists, and therefore has no feelings to be hurt. I con-fess that I find that old-world, roast-beef Anglicanism rather appealing. "Though Wiseman and Dullman combine against

Newman'', Barham wrote; and died four months too early to hear about Newman's change of religion. He is of his period.

Will he live? He could make the past live, in his own mannered way. Listen to this: "Now, thunder and turf, Pope Gregory said, (And his hair raised his triple crown right off his head), Now, thunder and turf, and out and alas, A horrible thing hath come to pass! What! cut off the head of Reverend Prior, and say he was *only* a bare-footed friar! What baron or squire or knight of the shire Is half so good as a holy friar? O turpissime! Vir nequissime! Sceleratissime, -quissime, -issime! Never, I trow, have the servi servorum Had before 'em Such a breach of decorum, Such a gross violation of morum bonorum!'' Those lines, quoted from memory after I shudder to think how many years, were written by a man who knew how to distribute his emphasis.

He will live, I hope, not as a period-piece, underscored with learned footnotes about the contemporary allusions; but as a boys' book, meant to be sprawled over on the hearth-rug, at an age when you like metres that carry you friskily along, and full-page pictures of the devil. I do not see why boys should not be reading him in 2045; and when those boys grow up, they will still be incapable of coming across a copy of the *Legends* without wanting to open it. Opening it, they will greet it not with Victorian cackles, but with a sigh, almost equally enjoyable, over the memories of their youth.

THE MAN WHO TRIED TO
CONVERT THE POPE

MOST of us are aware that, at intervals during the last
three centuries, efforts have been made by well-
meaning persons to realise the pathetic dream of a
reunited Church, something not quite Protestant and not
quite Catholic, based upon those principles of compromise
which are so dear to the English heart. But none of them, I
suppose, has ever been made with so little appreciation of the
facts, so quaint a misunderstanding of values, as that described
by its author in a book entitled *Journal of a Tour in Italy in 1850*,
by George Townsend, D.D., Canon of Durham, published by
Messrs. Rivington in 1851.

I am suspected, I do not know why, of being infected with
that April Fool's Day spirit which delights to palm off literary
frauds on the public. Let me explain, then, that the volume
really exists, and that my quotations are all genuine. Nor let
it be supposed that I am the victim, any more than I am the
author, of an imposture. Canon Townsend has his niche in the
Dictionary of National Biography; he is no fiction of a Tractarian
humorist, he is solid fact. A visit to Durham might even
supply us with his portrait, but I have felt the pilgrimage to
be unnecessary. I think I see the old gentleman well enough
as it is; white-chokered, well-tailored, earnest, whiskered
after the fashion of his time. He had got his canonry, I suppose,
before 1840, and was not therefore affected by the findings of
the Ecclesiastical Commission, which cut down its value to a
beggarly thousand a year; he liked, clearly, to do himself well,
and was not infected with the enthusiasm of the Evangelicals.

But the Oxford Movement has equally passed him by; he was a Low Churchman of the old school, a complete fundamentalist in his attitude towards the Bible—as who was not, in his day? —and an Englishman *à outrance*. How did such a man condescend to take an interest in the corrupt politics of the Vatican, or the insanitary population of the Seven Hills?

I think it was due to an odd streak of logic in his composition, which drove him on from strength to strength, regardless of prudent counsels, and shaking of heads in high places. He realised, it seems, that the numerous prayers which an Anglican has to offer up in the course of his ministry for the welfare and guidance of the Universal Church cannot be said with any real meaning when your practical interest is centred entirely in the national church of one people, sparsely represented even in its dominions overseas. He wanted to do something about it; to establish an effective contact between the Christianity of his own country and Christianity on the other side of the Channel; and his sublime confidence in the rightness of his own position convinced him that there was only one course open—he must persuade the erring Christians of the Continent to change their minds. How he took the first steps in this direction had best be described in his own words:

Ten years have elapsed since I commenced a laborious work on the Pentateuch, entitled "Scriptural Communion with God". The sixth and final part was completed at the end of last year (1849) immediately before I left England for Italy. As the reunion of Christians, or the establishment of the truth, unity and concord for which we pray, by unpoperizing the Church of Rome, was the frequent subject of my private prayers to God, the meditations on which those prayers were founded were embodied in various dedications, prefixed to the last four parts of that work. The third part was dedicated to Pope Gregory the XVIth. It related to the mode in which the work of the reunion of Christians might be commenced . . . that as laws must be rescinded by the powers which enact them, and as the bulls of Popes have frequently been rescinded by their successors, the bull, therefore, which decreed that twelve doctrines be added to the Nicene Creed, as articles of faith, may be rescinded by the present Pope, or by any of his successors, without propounding any condemnation of the articles themselves. If this was done, the propositions which the Council of Trent commended to the approbation of the Roman Catholic Church might be reconsidered in another Council, summoned under the authority of Christian temporal princes, of whom the Bishop of Rome might be one; and in this mode the hope of a better state of Christianity might dawn upon the world.

The fourth part of the book was dedicated in the same sense to the sovereigns of Europe, the fifth to Queen Victoria, and the sixth to the Universal Episcopate. "And the Dedication is concluded with the words of the despair with which I was conscious that I might as well have spoken to the dead themselves, for the present time at least"—he was addressing the Archbishop of Canterbury—"Can your Grace do nothing— nothing to remove the mutual hatred of Christians?"

It does not appear that either Gregory XVI or Queen Victoria, or Dr. Sumner, made any reply to these overtures. The Pope must have been on his death-bed, I imagine, when his volume appeared. Queen Victoria was much occupied at the time with the cares of the nursery, and the remaining secular princes of Europe were mostly hurled from their thrones by the revolutions of 1848. Archbishop Sumner did not want to hear the word Rome mentioned at all; it was but a year or two since Newman had made his submission, and a storm was already brewing over the Gorham controversy which was to determine the ecclesiastical career of Arch-deacon Manning. In fact, there could hardly have been a less opportune moment for Canon Townsend's activities; but the more distracted the state of Europe, the more confident he felt that the summoning of a new Council, to supersede and undo the Council of Trent, was the only remedy for every disorder.

At this point fate intervened. The labour of educing six volumes of spiritual consolation from the sometimes arid material of Leviticus and Deuteronomy could not but tell upon the constitution of the writer, though he were a man so tough of fibre as Canon Townsend. A change of scene and climate was the doctor's ultimatum—we are in the period when it was fashionable to recommend the Grand Tour. At first, the patient demurred; then a salutary thought struck him. Why not consent to travel, and make this the excuse for a personal interview with the head of the corrupt Roman Church?

"I would proceed to the Vatican," he says—Canon Town-send is always sonorous in his phraseology—"and seek an audience of the Pope, whom I had so often addressed from a distance, as an almost imaginary personage; I would appeal to him . . . to begin, and to commend by his great authority, the reconsideration of the past. In proportion to my magnificent independence, should be my extreme and deferential courtesy. In proportion to my zeal to serve the cause of peace, on the basis of Truth, should be my caution never to offend. The very attempt to gain admission to the Vatican would subject me, I well knew, to the charge of enthusiasm, fanaticism, and folly . . . I well knew, that disinterestedness is always folly, in the opinion of the selfish, the formal, and the dull."

A man who could thus imitate the style of Gibbon was not likely to be put off, it is clear, by any ordinary dissuasions.

But one curious difficulty he did experience. A stickler for the methods of primitive Christianity, as exemplified in St.

Paul's Epistles, he felt it would not be etiquette to demand an audience at the Vatican without a recommendation from some bishop nearer home. And this, he complains, was prohibited by the laws of his country. I find it difficult to believe that if Dr. Sumner had furnished the Canon with letters of introduction, either of them would have been prosecuted under the act of King Henry VIII in restraint of appeals. I fancy the true difficulty lay rather in the Archbishop's attitude towards the journey; I cannot resist quoting Dr. Townsend's account of it, because it is so beautiful a model of the attitude adopted by all Archbishops of Canterbury on all similar occasions.

> My venerable friend the Archbishop of Canterbury, though he declined to comply with my request that I might use his name, in the most general manner, as one desirous of the peace of the Church, when I should see the Bishop of Rome; and though he discouraged rather than encouraged my persevering, expressed to me, in his answer to my request, every kind and friendly wish.

That was all very well, but it was hardly a Pauline recommendation. Thereupon, Canon Townsend devised a scheme which does remarkable credit to his ingenuity. He would go over to Paris, call on the British Ambassador, get an introduction from him to the Cardinal Archbishop, and so extract from the Cardinal Archbishop the fortifying documents he needed. He realised, like others who have undertaken similar errands before and since his time, that an Englishman who goes round leaving cards, instead of sitting about in the lounge of his hotel, always goes down well on the Continent. Canon Townsend had little honour in his own country; Monsieur le Chanoine would carry all before him in the polite society of France.

There was a further difficulty which does not seem to have

daunted him as it might have daunted the modern peace-maker. He had received, no doubt, an excellent public school education; but in those days there was no School Certificate; he could not speak a word of Italian, or a word of French. But he had a resource here of which neither the Archbishop of Paris nor the Pope of Rome could boast. Mrs. Townsend must have been a remarkable woman; I am sorry that her husband's reticence makes it so difficult to form a distinct picture of her. But though there was no Somerville in those days, and no Girton, it is clear that she talked both French and Italian without difficulty. Had not Canon Townsend a right to carry about with him a sister, a wife, like the Apostles? Certainly he had, and I think it is quite possible that he would have found it difficult to organise the expedition without her. As she had got to go, she would come in very handy as an interpreter.

For the rest, her husband rightly argued that, if he talked his best school Latin to foreign ecclesiastics, they must at least show a polite affectation of understanding him. It is clear that he used this method a good deal. Between Valence and Avignon, for example, he travelled with a priest who, to his evident surprise, was "neither vulgar nor slovenly in his appearance, nor sheepish in his looks or demeanour", and he opened up at once with the phrase "Intelligisne Latinam, Domine?" The only trouble was the difference of pronunciation. Canon Townsend gives it as his opinion that "the Continental pronunciation of the Greek is better, and of the Latin worse, than our own." But, whether it was better or worse, it was inevitable that a man who read Latin "as spelt" should tax the patience of his Continental interlocutors. However, he seems to have got on well enough. He did not, I think, make the mistake of adopting unnecessarily Ciceronian turns of phrase; his Latin was of a more pedestrian order. Thus, when his cabman pursued him into the cathedral at

Naples, complaining that he had not received his full fare, the Canon ordered payment to be made, and explained to the priest who was awaiting him "Ecclesia non locus est controversiae", a sentiment which was excellently received.

It was, then, in the guise of an ordinary English tourist, anxious to learn what these damn foreigners look like when they are at home, that Canon Townsend set out on his memorable journey. To the last, his friend Dr. Gilly, the historian and advocate of the Vaudois, tried to dissuade him. He records, under January 22nd, the day of his sailing, the ineffectiveness of these protests.

> If God could make Saul the persecutor Paul the Apostle, God can make the Bishop of Rome himself the opponent of the old Popery. Modern experience shall not destroy my faith that, in spite of all present appearances, men shall be one fold under the great Shepherd. I will never sacrifice Truth, but I will persevere to speak peace, as the will of Christ, and of God. Wednesday. the 23rd. Arrived at Meurice's Hotel in Paris, where we had previously ordered apartments.

It must be confessed that our hero did not emulate the unkempt appearance or the fanatical deportment of earlier agitators, like Peter the Hermit. He travelled in style, with at least two servants, I am not certain of the exact number, to wait upon himself and Mrs. Townsend. And from the first he used, and found himself justified in using, the methods of a feudal class. Lord Brougham was staying at Meurice's, and Canon Townsend was well dug in with Lord Brougham. For Lord Brougham, it appears, had made some utterances in the celebrated case of King *v*. Williams which were unacceptable to the clergy; when he came to Durham, therefore, on circuit, the other canons did not ask him to dine; but, with a providential broadmindedness, Canon Townsend did.

At eleven o'clock, the earliest hour permissible by the customs of society, I called upon Lord Brougham. The conversation was animated and interesting.

What Lord Brougham thought we do not know, but he promised to provide letters. And at eleven the next morning Canon Townsend was round again.

At eleven I was with him, and, while he breakfasted, renewed the conversation of the preceding day. After a lively and interesting conversation on Wycliffe, and the ecclesiastical history of the Middle Ages . . . his Lordship gave me some letters of introduction to his friends at Rome. "I am not acquainted," he added, "with Pio Nono nor with the Archbishop of Paris, but here is a letter to the Marquis of Normanby" (then Ambassador in Paris) "and most sincerely do I wish you success in your" (and he added some words of eulogy) "mission."

Next day the Canon is at Lord Normanby's. He "observed that he read Lord Brougham's writing with some difficulty, as it was very peculiar, but that he saw something in the letter that referred to my going to Rome". Poor Lord Normanby! He should have been more careful. As it was, he got a long allocution, in which the Canon explained his intentions in full detail. Under this treatment, like everybody else who met Canon Townsend, he succumbed; he would write a letter of introduction to the Archbishop of Paris. But he warned our hero to be careful.

He informed me that at the present juncture there prevailed at Rome a great deal of jealousy on the subject of conversion; that any attempt in that direction would be looked upon with much suspicion.

Canon Townsend remained unperturbed.

I told his Lordship that my object, in one sense, was not conversion; that, in the commonly understood sense, I did not intend to put myself forward as the opponent of Popery . . .

and so on, and so on, till Lord Normanby hastily agreed to see the Archbishop of Paris himself, and let Canon Townsend know the result.

The next day was Sunday. Lord Brougham called, with eye bandaged as the result of an accident, to say good-bye; it was due to this accident, he explained, that he was forced to travel on the Lord's Day. "We wished him a pleasant journey, and a useful life." Let it not be supposed from this that Canon Townsend was lax about Sunday observance. Here are his impressions of the Continental Sunday:

> If we had not been grieved and shocked, we should have been amused by the vivacity of the people in the streets, whom we passed on our way. They seem to imagine that religion being a very dull, uninteresting matter, they must chase away its dullness by external and most intense gaiety. They seem to be utterly ignorant of the delightful fact that a Christian's duty is a Christian's privilege, and that to keep the Lord's Day holily is only to keep the Lord's Day happily, to increase inward felicity, and to anticipate the pleasures of the immortality that is before us.

"If we had not been grieved and shocked, we should have been amused"; what more appropriate description of the Englishman in Paris? But I must not linger too much over Canon Townsend's impressions of Travel. It is enough to say that he faithfully admires every building, picture and view which his guide-book recommends to his admiration, but seldom without some melancholy reflections upon the local representatives of the human species, their ignorance of the Bible, and their superstitious veneration for the Virgin Mary.

The interview with Mgr. Sibour, then Archbishop of Paris, took place on the following Saturday. The interpreter was a gentleman not named, but described as "the former Roman Catholic correspondent of *The Times*". Canon Townsend appears to have been particularly careful on this occasion to observe his own principles of "caution never to offend". He wanted letters to the Pope, he said, that he might converse with him on the expediency of summoning, in conjunction with other sovereigns, another General Council. No word is spoken of the interdicted Bible or of the twelve articles added to the Creed by the corrupt Council of Trent. The Archbishop, however, seems to have scented an equivocation about the term "Council", and asked on what principle Monsieur wished to see it assemble? The Canon talked vaguely about common Christianity and a common danger from the infidels; he referred to the negotiations in Queen Anne's time between Dupin and Archbishop Wake. Mgr. Sibour's next question was an unexpected one. "And", said he, "is Monsieur a Puseyite?" Canon Townsend has vividly depicted for us his annoyance.

"I was sorry", he says, "to be thought to have touched that pitch, and to be defiled with the touch; I was sorry to be regarded as one of those imbeciles, who imagine that either Christian peace or Christian holiness can be restored to the universal Church by bringing the Church of England into conformity with the Church of Rome", etc., etc.

But he does not seem to have expressed his horror in very outspoken terms. All he said was, "I am an Episcopalian Christian, and I can assume nor bear no other appellation." It is doubtful whether the Archbishop was much enlightened; however, he promised the letters of recommendation to the Holy Father, and, sure enough, on the following Tuesday they arrived. In a fortnight Canon Townsend was off to Rome, with the key to the Vatican in his pocket.

By diligence all the way to Lyons, by steamer from Lyons to Avignon. At Valence he finds a golden inscription to Pio Nono; "this marble monument," he says to himself, "with its inscription, shall be to me an omen of the reception I shall experience, and of the probability of the useful or useless results of my mission. I read the inscription. It was the memorial of the gratitude of the canons of the cathedral of Valence to Pio Nono; for what, I exclaimed, for what reason is the gratitude? I could with difficulty believe the evidence of my senses, when I read that the gratitude of the Canons of Valence to Pio Nono was here commemorated, because he had permitted the bowels of his predecessor, who had died at Valence, to rest here, while the body was conveyed for its burial to Rome! . . . What would be thought or said in England, if the Canons of Winchester had raised a memorial to Bishop Sumner, because he permitted them to retain the bowels of Bishop Tomline, while his body was buried at St. Paul's? If this act would be deemed absurd in England, why not in Italy?"

Quite so, quite so; only somehow Bishop Tomline does make it funnier.

Undeterred by the sinister omens which the entrails provided for him, Canon Townsend pressed on for Rome. He went from Marseilles to Genoa by sea; for the rest, he was dependent on the diligence, and it was not till the twentieth, after four weeks of travel, that he set foot in the city. The time of his arrival was hardly propitious. For more than a year Pius IX had been absent from the city, owing to a popular insurrection, and it was not many months since French troops had entered the capital to restore order there. The Pope was still in Naples, and the date of his return uncertain. The English Consul recommended that Canon Townsend should proceed to Naples at once, without communicating his plan or his desire to anyone at Rome. This was too much to expect; nor did our hero's good fortune desert him. He made friends with Father Mesaheb, a Maronite Jesuit from Mount Lebanon —so at least he is described—was taken round by him, argued freely with him on theological points, and secured an introduction from him to the antiquarian, Cardinal Mai. The interview proceeded on the now familiar lines. Latin was spoken, with interpreters present in case Italian were needed.

> He bowed, and permitted me to proceed, as I had done with the Archbishop of Paris, I fear at some length, to submit to him the object of my visit to Rome . . . [etc.]

The Cardinal seems to have insisted chiefly on the practical difficulties of summoning an international council to discuss the danger of infidelity and Socialism in the then state of affairs. But he took all the Canon's views in good part, and when, before leaving, his visitor pointed to some English books with the observation, "it could not be expected that the nation which had produced such works could ever again be submissive to Rome", contented himself with replying *Paulatim*.

> He was evidently . . . impressed with the conviction, which seemed indeed to be general among his brethren, that England was returning to the adoption of the Papal additions to the faith of Christ. I sighed at the mistake, and again expressed my conviction and my hope that this could never be; and he said again with emphasis, *Paulatim*.

There is something pathetically typical, in that troubled Rome of 1850, about the Canon's haste for action and the Cardinal's readiness to wait upon the future. They parted good friends, with a warm invitation to Cardinal Mai to come and stay at Durham any time when he was evicted from his country. They exchanged letters, on which Canon Townsend comments, "The only stumbling-block between us is this steady, invincible determination never to be reformed." He found, as others have found before and since, how difficult it is to arrive at a complete agreement with a man who will not adopt your own point of view.

It is actually on record that our canon visited St. Peter's on a Sunday morning. "Can I keep the Sabbath, or Lord's Day, holy, by going there? Yes, I wish to see how the common Lord of the Sabbath is honoured by those who assume to be more peculiarly His servants." The sermon was "upon the whole, unobjectionable", but the line must be drawn somewhere. "I could not kneel at the elevation of the Host." It must not be supposed that his sturdy Protestantism was ever stampeded by its alien surroundings. He was visited by one of the English converts—I wonder which? He was not impressed: "Discussion in conversation, when there is but little or no previous reading, becomes tedious." He is invited to attend the consecration of Cullen as Primate of Ireland; "I refused to sanction the insult to my Church and country." More profitably, he consents to perform a wedding service in the Lutheran chapel.

One of the princesses of Prussia had given a very beautiful covering for the altar, and had adorned it, in the most elaborate gold embroidery, with a grouping of the Cross, an anchor, and flowers. I congratulated the company present . . . and reminded them that the flowers of life most abounded in beauty and fragrance when they were blended with a good hope of the future and entwined round the Cross . . . Much enthusiasm was kindled by a few observations of this nature, and the Lord's Day was not desecrated, though all was cheerfulness, and joyousness, and smiles.

But he remained true to his purpose of working for reunion, and, when taken to task by some gentlemen of the Scottish Free Church, represented to them that, though some supporters of Popery might justly be called serpents and a generation of vipers, "this could not be said of all".

On Friday, the 12th of April, the Pope returned to the city, amid the eager expectations of a large crowd, which knelt to receive his blessing, and of Canon Townsend, who bowed. On the 13th an audience was solicited; on the 25th, word was received that the Holy Father would receive Signor Townsend the following day in private audience, "unitamente alla Consorte". In just over three months the indomitable peacemaker had triumphed over every obstacle, and stood on the threshold of his great enterprise. There were minor regrets; the Italian gentleman who was to have interpreted was unable to be present, but Mrs. Townsend readily volunteered to supply his place; and again

> I was sorry that I had not with me my academic dress. My wearing the robes of an English clergyman would have been but the more proper observance of the courtesy which was due to the Pope as a temporal Prince, and as the Bishop of the greatest of the Western Churches. I assumed the usual evening dress required by society in England.

At half-past five they were ushered into the presence. Why Pio Nono should have been dressed in "the long white fine cloth Dominican robe" or wearing the "Dominican cap on his head", I am unable to discover. He received them alone with the utmost graciousness, asked Mrs. Townsend whether she had been to Italy before, whether she admired the country, what objects in Rome had interested her most, in what language her husband desired to converse? Then the Canon was let loose; not, he hastens to assure us, in a speech, but in answer to the Pope's questions. He asked for a General Council of Christians, at which the Pope was to have precedence, though not jurisdiction. The usual practical difficulties were urged in reply. There was no discussion of details.

> It has been said, I know not why, that I alluded to the celibacy of the clergy, and the giving of the cup to the laity. I said nothing of the kind.

We learn from another passage that Mrs. Townsend understood Latin; apart from that, it is quite clear that the Canon did not mean to suggest any programme of reform for the Roman Church until the Council should be already in session. He presented a document for the Pope to read, enshrining his appeal. "I am a Protestant," he explained, "and I have always been an enemy to your Church, but there will not be found in this document any expression which will be personally offensive."

Mrs. Townsend hastened to reassure the Holy Father about this: "No, no, mio marito è troppo buono" and so on. Many Christians in England, the Canon explained, would rejoice in the hope of the reunion of the Churches. I cannot find that he had much authority for this remark, for it appears that all his friends had discouraged the expedition. But it did service on this occasion as on others. "Yes," said Pio Nono, "there are in England many persons of good will" "There are many good men there who would rejoice in peace," replies the Canon, and explains in a footnote that the Pope was quoting from a false text of the New Testament when he talked about "men of good will". All modern scholarship, I fear, is against Canon Townsend and with the Pope on this point. Asked whether he knew Dr. Wiseman, our hero cautiously explained that he lived in retirement, and was not personally known to him. Then, after a forty minutes' interview, the intrepid couple took their leave, bowing themselves out as if from the presence of the Queen. Some Cubans who were admitted after them "both knelt down, as to God. . . . We had not done so. We had rendered every respect to the Pope as to an earthly sovereign; we could not venerate him as our God".

The text of the memorandum left with the Pope is then given. It defines the object of the Council, "restoring to the Catholic Church the ancient discipline and the primitive union", but says nothing about the Council of Trent, or the twelve popish additions to the Nicene Creed. In fact, it is a document which Dr. Pusey might have written, and I suspect that Pio Nono took the Canon for a Tractarian. We learn, on the authority of an English gentleman who had an interview soon afterwards, that he thought the *Canone di Durham* an excellent and good man, but found his Latin difficult to follow; "he did not think the proposal of summoning a Council would lead to the desired effect". And here a misunderstanding seems to have arisen. The Canon had a visit next day from Monsignor de Mérode and Dr. Grant, of the English college, who told him that "His Holiness had read my memorial, and desired to converse with me further on the subject of its contents".

It would appear, from what followed, that a mere polite expression of interest was somehow misconstrued into a summons for a fresh audience. It was with that hope that Canon Townsend left for Naples, promising to wait on the Holy Father on his way home.

I have no space to describe that splendid visit to Naples; how they were shewn round the Cathedral sacristy, and Mrs. Townsend was not allowed to touch the chalices, though her husband was, on her assurance that he was a Canon too; how they attended the liquefaction of St. Januarius's blood—the Canon, under the impression that Mr. Neumann, a chemist of

Berlin, had reproduced the alleged miracle in his own laboratory, saw the liquefaction perfectly, and bears witness to it. When they returned to Rome they found that the Pope was not expecting a fresh discussion with them, and did not like, on their side, to press for a second interview, since there was naturally a great press of business at the Vatican. Accordingly, on the 27th of May, they set out from Rome on their homeward journey.

Did Canon Townsend feel that he had failed? I think not, at the time. It is clear that there was one Catholic doctrine of which he had no appreciation—he did not realize that the decisions of a Council are irreformable. He thought of a Council—he uses the parallel himself—as if its decisions could always be changed later on, like the decisions of an English Parliament. And he believed, or at least tried to persuade himself, that a new General Council would find no more difficulty about repudiating Transubstantiation than a Labour Government might have about dropping the artificial silk duties.

But there are other passages, scattered throughout the book, which talk the language of despair. I do not like the methods of those critics who profess to find traces of different documentary strata in Canon Townsend's beloved Pentateuch. But I confess that I am inclined to apply the method to his own *Journal*, and suggest that these defeatist passages were put in later, when the book was preparing for the press, in the light of subsequent events. Both at Rome and at Naples he observes the volcanic character of the soil, and speculates whether Dr. Cumming is not right in supposing that the whole of the south of Italy, from Rome to Naples, is shortly to be destroyed by fire.

Oh, for that warning voice, which he who saw the Apocalypse heard cry in heaven, that I might be heard in my appeal to the Bishop of Rome when I say, Repent, Repent, rescind your additions to the religion of Jesus Christ!

But Dr. Townsend *had* seen the Pope, and did not say anything of the kind. Again, as he looks back on Rome on leaving it, he breaks out into a tremendous denunciation of Rome, and of the traitorous spirits in England who encourage its pretensions.

> Go on, Church of Rome. The divisions of England strengthen thee! The traitors of England love thee, and give thee power. Fill up the measure of thy ancient iniquity. Send out the unrequired bishops to insult us, the unrequired priests to mock us. Go on! The government is indifferent, the people are torpid, the Church is silent.

And much more to the same effect. Now, why should a clergyman who has gone out to Rome to promote unity in Christendom, who has been received with the utmost kindness by an archbishop, two cardinals and the Pope himself, all of whom are content to point out that the time is not ripe just yet for the summoning of a General Council—why should such a man feel, as he leaves the city, so deep-rooted a grievance against its inhabitants?

The answer is that he did not feel it at the time; he put that part in afterwards. He went back to England with the consciousness that his memorandum lay on the table in the Vatican, wondering what reply it would provoke. On September 29th, little more than two months after his return, a bull was issued restoring the English hierarchy, and on October 7th Wiseman issued his pastoral from the Flaminian Gate. Poor Canon Townsend! Here was his journal, I take it, already advertised and undergoing its final process of polishing, with all the nice things he said about popes and cardinals, and all the nice things popes and cardinals said about him; and then suddenly, this official insult to Lambeth, this gratuitous affront to the feelings of Protestant England. He did the best he could; he put his journal into shape, let in a few passages to emphasise the hard-heartedness and all-but irreformability of Rome; then he sent it to the press, tacking on at the beginning a preface in which he lets himself go.

It is a strange preface to such a work. He explains that the journal was written, with the exception of a few sentences, "long before the promulgation of the late unscriptural, absurd and insolent bull of the Pope, whom I visited at the Vatican". He expresses the hope that the Papists of the Continent will be brought to their senses by a fresh reformation. But how is this to be secured? By resisting papal aggression in England. The resistance, he assures us, must be of three kinds, Political, Christian and Ecclesiastical. First, by way of political resistance, we must repeal the Acts of Catholic Emancipation. Next, by way of Christian resistance, we must maintain our protest; our motto must be, No peace with Rome. I do not understand what he means by ecclesiastical opposition, and I am very doubtful if he did himself; the fact is, Canon Townsend was rattled.

> If I could have imagined the possibility of the folly and crime which the Pope has committed, I would never have entered Rome.

It would be possible to point or at least to suggest, all sorts of morals as a tail-piece to Canon Townsend's story. I prefer to leave it without comment, as the story of an honest Englishman who really did set out to do great things on his holiday, really did think that he could turn the Grand Tour into a grand slam, and failed so unexpectedly. He lived to 1857; he was not permitted, therefore, to see the summoning of the Council which he recommended, or to mourn the definition of Infallibility which was its principal result. And somewhere, I suppose, in the débris of the Vatican archives lies his memorandum to the Pope, all written fair in Italian, a document of our mortality, and a warning, should it ever be needed, to some new generation which has forgotten it.

THE BARSETSHIRE NOVELS

THOSE of us who can boast that we loved Trollope a generation ago, long before his almost unprecedented return to public favour, usually mean, if we will be honest with ourselves, that we loved Barsetshire. Not that you can write him off as *homo sex librorum*; but it is by a single group of his works that he stands or falls—if a man "does not see anything" in *Framley Parsonage*, there is no more to be said. It was the publication of *The Warden* in 1855 that first brought Trollope fame; within two years after the publication of *The Last Chronicle* in 1867, his fame began to decline. And during the long years of occultation, you would meet a hundred people who had heard of Mrs. Proudie for every one who had heard of Burgo Fitzgerald. Refuse, if you will, to put the Barsetshire novels on a separate pedestal; you must still put them in a separate category.

Trollope's "clerical" novels have a principle of unity to which his political novels make no claim—unity of place. The world of *Phineas Finn* is real to us only because it is inhabited by the same set of people, and they are all interested in the same kind of thing. But *Doctor Thorne* does not reintroduce us to any of the characters we met in *Barchester Towers*, except the De Courcy lot; nor does the tentative sacerdotalism of Mr. Oriel amount to anything more than a whiff of incense. It is the medical, not the clerical world of Barchester that comes and goes. Yet we know where we are, because there are familiar names on every sign-post. By an extraordinary piece of magic Trollope, alone among our novelists, has enriched England with a forty-first county. Nothing could be more unexpected; Trollope had no eye for scenery, and did not begin to notice things till he was inside your front gate. A carpet-bagger, if ever there was one, Trollope is for ever carrying off his readers to Scotland or Ireland, or even taking them for a Mediterranean cruise—it was in the Near East, actually, that he wrote *Doctor Thorne*. Only in Barsetshire did he find a home wicket; for his readers, as for himself, it acquires the same kind of objectivity which belongs to Sherlock Holmes or Mr. Pickwick. Even in *The Small House at Allington*, though we are in a different county, it is the next county, and Courcy Castle lies in fatal proximity.

He had stumbled on fairyland by accident. Notoriously, he himself claimed that Barchester was Winchester, not Salisbury or Wells, although he was prepared to admit (as if it were a thing of no consequence) that the county lay farther west. Ullathorne Court could only be appreciated by those who "know something of the glories of Wiltshire, Dorsetshire and Somersetshire";[1] and Lady de Courcy, in what is plainly a catalogue of local *mésalliances*, draws attention to the fate of "young Mr. Everbeery, near Taunton".[2] But in *The Warden* he had no intention of creating a county. The only place visited, outside Barchester and London, is the Archdeacon's rectory at Plumstead; the name is perhaps an echo from Somerset, from Huish Episcopi, but the description given is deliberately unfriendly. There is nothing to show that greater things are in the germ, Ullathorne, and Greshamsbury, and Framley, and Courcy, and Chaldicotes.

Indeed, *The Warden* gives promise of nothing beyond itself. It was conceived as a satire, by an author whom nature had not designed for a satirist. Trollope had a robust dislike of shams and abuses, an equally robust dislike of the glib reformer; and he admits that in *The Warden* he attempted the impossible feat of satirizing both parties to a dispute at once. The funds of St. Cross Hospital at Winchester had, so the newspapers

[1] *Barchester Towers*, ch. 22.   [2] *Doctor Thorne*, ch. 6.

said, been maladministered; and Trollope did not know whether to be more angry with the Church for having maladministered them, or with the newspapers for having said so. He attacked, simultaneously, the Church and the Press; the second part of his moral was the more noticeable, since it is common form in novels to attack the Church. People complained that the burlesque of Carlyle and of Dickens was a poor affair; the idols of a day are not easily dethroned. Actually, the parody of Carlyle is not bad, and the criticism of Dickens not undeserved. What really upsets the balance of the book is its anti-clericalism; there was no reason why the Archdeacon should keep a copy of Rabelais in a locked drawer, why one of his sons should have been nicknamed "Soapy", in undisguised allusion to a well-known bishop. Either attack might have proved successful, but not both. You cannot horsewhip two people at the same time.

Two things redeem the book from failure—the melodramatic but moving role assigned to Eleanor, and the character of Mr. Harding. Designed, perhaps, merely as a foil to show up the arrogance of the clergy by contrast, Mr. Harding became a favourite with his author, and it was perhaps a reluctance to leave his story unfinished that gave the world *Barchester Towers*. Trollope, more than most authors, was a bad judge of his own works, but he could not fail to realize that Mr. Harding was a creation. So sensitive a conscience, impressed by the world's judgments not from any tinge of worldliness, but because the world's judgments were its own mirror; so much mild obstinacy, that could hold its own in defiance of arguments which it could not meet, of dominant characters whom it was powerless to face—all *that* was a human being, real as Barsetshire is real, and deserved, no less than Barsetshire, an encore. If Mr. Harding was capable of resigning the hospital, he was capable of refusing the deanery; he had not said his last word yet.

By a fortunate chance, a craftsman may be able to fashion something worth while out of his own waste material, as when the arms of an ivory crucifix take shape for themselves out of the parings left over from the tusk. And, in something the same way, authors have been able before now to produce a living character out of what was meant to be a mere accessory, a mere foil. Pinkerton in *The Wrecker* was perhaps invented as a foil to the amiable *fainéance* of Loudon Dodd, and it was only a desire to set off the inhuman cleverness of Sherlock Holmes that produced Dr. Watson. Mr. Harding—himself, as has been suggested, a foil for certain unamiable clerical characteristics —had to be set off by contrast with another clergyman; and he, Archdeacon Grantly, became a living figure in his turn, though not, take him for all in all, unamiable. There is, to be sure, no subtlety about him; no psychology to be compared with the psychology of his father-in-law. But he has become an institution; we long for his appearance because we know exactly what to expect of him. We know that he is always destined to be a spoke in the wheel, but a friendly, a well-meaning spoke. Do not be deceived by his portrait in *The Warden*; by the secret volume of Rabelais, by the ungracious triumph over a repentant John Bold; all that was but the raw material of the Archdeacon. In the first chapter of *Barchester Towers*, when he sat by the death-bed of his father the Bishop, wondering whether death would come before the ministry went out, he won Trollope over. The two shook hands, and he was a changed man thenceforward. An ogre, to be sure; an ogre to his sister-in-law and to Grace Crawley (not to mention Lord Dumbello), but an ogre with his heart in the right place. That is part of his creator's genius; by the same right as Lady Lufton, the Archdeacon is an ogre all the more effective because he is so companionable.

By now, Trollope had found fresh enemies to do his work for him. The two Proudies, bishop and bishopess, and their chaplain, Mr. Slope, belong to a school of worldly, place-hunting Low Churchmen who can no longer claim the honoured name of "Evangelical". For the Proudies, Trollope has no good word till you reach the *Last Chronicle*; for Mr. Slope, none at all. If he had weakened towards them, they would not have been such admirable figures of fun. Yet, with all his dislike of these, the new brooms, he is fair-minded enough to admit that there were abuses in the old order of things—witness Dr. Vesey Stanhope, and the extraordinary family which he brought up in his villa on Lake Como. Their introduction into the atmosphere of a Cathedral close is the making of the book; they were so useful to its author that he cannot help rather liking them, for all his deep disapproval. With Mr. Arabin, it is the other way round; Trollope loves him dearly, but as usual makes his hero something of a stick.

After such a resounding achievement, he must have been tempted to let well alone; the Barchester situation had now really worked itself out. But, to the comfort of posterity, Trollope found himself suffering from a nostalgia for Barsetshire. When he wrote *Doctor Thorne* he was on his travels, away from books; he could not remember that there was no "e" in Grantly, and only one "p" in Plumstead; it must be added that he fell into fatal errors about Barsetshire geography. But he was now committed to a series; the thing had become a habit with him. *Doctor Thorne* is probably his best book, certainly his best plot—though in a sense it was not his; he tells us that it was presented to him by his brother. Its chief contribution to the saga of the county is, beyond doubt, Miss Dunstable. Trollope hated vulgarity, distrusted the *arriviste*, more than most authors. But Miss Dunstable, with her extraordinary faculty for making herself at home everywhere, sailed straight into Trollope's heart, with her companion, her pert doctor, her parrot and her poodle complete. She was too good to be dropped; and so we got *Framley Parsonage*.

But Miss Dunstable and the Greshams are not the only link which binds *Framley Parsonage* to *Doctor Thorne*. In a sense, it is the same story retold. This also is characteristic of Barsetshire, that the same patterns recur in it, almost as familiar as the sign-posts themselves. When Mr. Crawley is tricked into accepting a lift from Farmer Mangle, on his famous visit to the palace, we get that curious clairvoyant feeling that all this has happened before. The memory which is really disturbing us is that of Mrs. Quiverful, also bound for the palace, invoking the aid of Farmer Subsoil. When Johnny Eames attacks Mr. Crosbie at Paddington, there is another echo from the past; Frank Gresham had horsewhipped Mr. Moffat for the same offence—by some trick of unconscious memory, Trollope has called Mr. Moffat Gustavus, and Mr. Crosbie Adolphus. Bertie Stanhope proposing to Eleanor so as to please Charlotte, Frank Gresham proposing to Miss Dunstable to please his mother, Nat Sowerby proposing, again to Miss Dunstable, by way of Mrs. Harold Smith—it is all the same pattern, somehow unspoiled for us by repetition. On a larger scale, it is no new thing when Lord Lufton succumbs to the bright eyes of Lucy Robarts, and she behaves perfectly, and the powers that rule at Framley are with difficulty overcome; it is the old story of Frank Gresham, and Mary Thorne, and Lady Arabella. Only, this time, it is more like Trollope; the melodrama has faded out, and you have a human situation instead. Lady Lufton is so infinitely more sympathetic than Lady Arabella; Lucy suffers from no disabilities of income or of blood. It all turns on the penetrating question, "Is she not insignificant?" Nor, I think, if Lucy had suddenly become a great heiress would the *châtelaine* of Framley have made the same vulgar *volte-face* as Lady Arabella. It was because Lucy nursed Mrs. Crawley through her illness that at last, unobtrusively but unmistakably, she signified.

With *Framley Parsonage*, Trollope climbs back into the

pulpit which he had abandoned since *The Warden*. The osten-
tatious contrast between Mr. Crawley and Mark Robarts is not
accidental; the book is meant to be a tract about a subject
which always haunted Trollope's mind, the unequal distri-
bution of clerical incomes. But he does not succeed in writing
a tract; his absorbing interest in human nature betrays him.
Mr. Crawley, who was perhaps only invented as a set-off to
Mark Robarts' wealth, comes to dominate his author's mind,
just as Mr. Harding did. He is splendidly alive; a heroic figure,
but with all the defects of his qualities, proud, obstinate, in-
considerate. For that very reason, he does not enforce the
author's moral so cogently as poor Mr. Quiverful. If Trollope
is felicitous in portraying the clergy, he is still more so in
portraying the wives of the clergy. It is to Mrs. Crawley, as
to Mrs. Robarts, that our sympathies go out.

Framley Parsonage came three years after *Doctor Thorne*, *The
Small House at Allington* three years later, *The Last Chronicle*
three years later again—so admirably was Trollope a creature
of routine. It almost looks as if *The Small House* had been
forced into the series *malgré lui*, merely because Trollope said
to himself "It's time we gave 'em another Barchester". To
be sure, we spend an uncomfortable week at Courcy; we
sample, for a moment, the cheerful loquacity of Mr. Harding,
the ominous silence of his granddaughter. But Allington is in
a different county; in a different diocese, we may suspect, and
a different hunt—if there was one. But there is worse than
that; the general character of the book does not quite conform
to type. The story is slow-moving, the plot thin, the interest
concentrated on a very few persons, the pathos too sustained;
Lord de Guest is the only quite convincing figure. Authentic
Trollope it may be, but it has not the *élan* of Barsetshire.

It may have been some consciousness of this which induced
Trollope, most regrettably, to make the next novel of his
series the last. By general admission *The Last Chronicle of*

Barset is one of his very best books; but what most endears it to us is a kind of sunset glory—it reflects, at a hundred angles, those other chronicles which preceded it. The mystification about the cheque is a breath of wind which keeps the story moving, but hardly an end in itself; Grace Crawley, the heroine, repeats the experience of Mary Thorne and Lucy Robarts, but in a less spirited way; the sub-plot, up in London, is frankly unreadable. What delights us is to see all the characters we loved come on to the stage, make their bows, and take their applause. Mr. Harding's death is worthy of his life; the Archdeacon is still impotently repressive, his wife still patiently critical of him; Mrs. Proudie vulgarly obtrusive, her husband a forlorn puppet; Eleanor Arabin, to the last, does the wrong thing from the right motives. Miss Dunstable, now Mrs. Thorne, is at her old tricks, impelling the hero to defy family opposition. Mr. Crawley is still unmanageable, his wife still labouring to manage him; Lady Lufton so kind, but so heavy-handed, the Robartses so helpful, but so ineffective; Griselda as beautiful as ever, and as boring. Johnny Eames is a little older, but still a fool, Crosbie still irreclaimably a cad, Lily Dale still unreasonably a spinster. Even the minor characters are true to type; Mr. Harding must not die without Dr. Filgrave (though to be sure he has lost an "l") to pronounce his medical epitaph, and what better piece of dialogue did Trollope ever write than Mr. Robarts and Mr. Oriel discussing Grace Crawley? "We think her a great beauty," says the Rector of Framley; "as for manners, I never saw a girl with a prettier way of her own." "Dear me," said Mr. Oriel. "I wish she had come to breakfast." Poor Mr. Oriel, so excellent and so comfortably off, yet always somehow missing the higher experiences!

Thus our author reassembles his characters, their destinies intertwined at last; a perfect mosaic, made up out of what we thought were brilliant chips from the master's workshop. So well trained are they by now, these Barsetshire folk, that each reacts effortlessly to the situation at a mere crack of the whip. Doubtless the question will always be debated, whether Mrs. Proudie was artistically killable. But, once her death-warrant was out, who else could have described the repercussions of it with such courageous realism? Nor can we be certain, on merely artistic grounds, that the stroke which fell on Mrs. Proudie was unpremeditated. We have all been brought up on the story of Trollope going home and finishing her off out of mere bravado, as the result of a chance remark made at the Club. But it is arguable that he "had it in for her" already. The story was designed to have a happy ending—a happy ending, not simply for Grace Crawley and her father, not only for Plumstead Rectory, but for a whole countryside. Barsetshire was to be left at peace, and what peace could there be, so long as—we must leave it to the Archdeacon to finish up the quotation. The Whig principle which first reared its head when John Bold took up the wrongs of Hiram's bedesmen has worked itself out. Mr. Slope has disappeared, and the Scatcherds, and Chaldicotes has been rescued from falling into the hands of the Duke. One focus of Whiggery remains, there in the palace. Let Mrs. Proudie be liquidated, and Barchester can return to the immemorial peace which it enjoyed at the beginning of *The Warden*; the epic cycle is complete.

That, after all, is the secret of Barsetshire; that is why it appeals to a nostalgic age like our own. It symbolizes the twilight of an *ancien régime*; a twilight which seemed to its contemporaries as though it might, perhaps, be only cloud. The reforms which belong to the first half of the nineteenth century had left their mark on English society, but as yet only an uncertain one, like ripples on the surface of a clear pool. Outwardly, the governing forces of English life seemed to remain what they were—the landed gentry, the Established

Church, the two ancient universities; and yet that world of privilege was threatened. For a moment, when he sketched out the plot of *The Warden*, Trollope half believed that he was on the side of the reformers. But when, in the first chapter of *Barchester Towers*, the Government went out just in time to secure the appointment of a Whig bishop, the die was cast; from that point onwards the series is an epic of reaction; all Trollope's heroes are Conservatives, all his villains are Whigs. In the political novels, politics are only a game; in the "clerical" novels all is in deadly earnest—every contested election, every vacant prebend, begins to matter. He could not save the old order of things, the world of privilege he so intimately loved, but his sympathies have embalmed the unavailing conflict.

Not that he will ever allow his characters to develop into a set of types, mere champions of the thing they stand for. And indeed, of all his clerical characters the one he loves best is the one he invented first, no champion at all, but a laggard, a skulker from the battle—that same Mr. Harding who made the *gran rifiuto* over Hiram's Hospital, and could even reconcile himself to the thought of having Mr. Slope for a son-in-law. All through the series the apologetic figure of the Precentor flits in and out, a man whose unaffected holiness acts as a kind of spirit-level by which the motives of other men can be gauged, even if they be as crooked as the motives of Adolphus Crosbie. Trollope seems more reluctant to make an end of his favourite than even of Mrs. Proudie—would not have done so, perhaps, if he had not wanted to create a vacancy and install Mr. Crawley as rector of St. Ewold's. (As a matter of fact, Mr. Harding never had been rector of St. Ewold's; but he had been so patient and contented ever since he lost the wardenship that Trollope quite thought he was.)[1] Of all the Barsetshire novels, *The Warden* is perhaps the least conclusive and

[1] *Barchester Towers*, last paragraph; cf. *The Last Chronicle of Barset*, ch. 36.

the least characteristic. But it is a fitting preface to the series, just because its hero is a man who contrives to stand outside all that epic of conflict; a man so essentially Christian that, if the world in general were like him, there would be no conflict at all.

R. L. STEVENSON

CAPTAIN DAVIS, when he played the accordion to the Kanakas, justified himself in the words "I've got to play something, though; got to pay the shot, my son". It is not to be supposed that he enjoyed it; indeed, he described himself afterwards as having danced for his breakfast like a poodle-dog. To me, too, the moment has come when I must earn my lunch—or rather, not earn it; a lunch like that is an uncovenanted mercy; but do something to pay my shot. Fluency I never had; I get to my feet unwillingly; I have not yet reached the years of Uncle Joseph, who would have travelled thirty miles to address an infant school. Yet speech is demanded of me. It is not merely that I have been lunching; that, as Michael Finsbury observes, is the sort of thing that may happen to any man. I am besides the guest of a society vowed to a certain niceness of literary taste, gourmets of exact prose; or how should you be met on such an anniversary, to invoke over your cups the gracious memory of Robert Louis Stevenson? For that, I am your debtor; and if I cannot pay the debt, honour demands I should declare my bankruptcy.

Strange, not that his laurels should endure, but that they should seem so fresh. Next year, it hardly bears thinking of, you will be celebrating a centenary. So long dead he is, and so little dated; Mallock, who was born in 1849, died a much older man than Stevenson, and Mallock is of yesterday. Perhaps what shortens the perspective of memory is that Stevenson is the companion of a lifetime; you pick up the habit in childhood, and you must be in your second childhood before you depart from it. For myself, I was already Stevenson-minded while he yet lived; I could not listen to *Treasure*

Island any more after the midnight terrors occasioned by Pew's death, but I ran about the school-room chanting "Yo-ho-ho and a bottle of rum" as truculently as my elder brothers. And still, of all modern authors, I find him most surely re-readable.

Is that a grudging tribute? Not from me. Let me seize upon this opportunity to make a confession, or to air a grievance—I hardly know which. Among all the detestable habits which make me angry with my contemporaries, and still more with my juniors, I know none worse than this; their habit of inventing new art-forms which make you ashamed of admiring the old. It was to be hoped that advancing years would fortify me with such a crust of conservatism as I have ever observed in my seniors; by the time I was sixty I would be prepared to dismiss all modern stuff as childish bungling. But no, if you have a distrust of your own judgment in such matters, the mere reiteration of what seemed nonsense when you first came across it makes it somehow impressive. Isn't Raphael, after all, rather chocolate-box? Doesn't the Hermes of Praxiteles, perhaps, answer to the description of Edinburgh Rock, or whatever may be the pejorative term in use among sculptors? Mark you, we older people get nothing in exchange; they cannot teach us to like Picasso, they cannot enable us to make head or tail—or body, for that matter—out of Epstein. No, the new idiom remains a closed book to us, and meanwhile we are a trifle out of conceit with our old favourites; something has tarnished our vision of them. Even the aspiring upward thrust of that older architecture looks a trifle strained, somehow a trifle mannered, when the eye has grown accustomed to street after street of modern flats all built sideways, like a Neapolitan ice. "Standing between two worlds, one dead, the other powerless to be born"—so Matthew Arnold put it; and yet, is even Matthew Arnold the inspired prophet we took him for, when we read him in our school-days, more than forty years ago?

I confess that when it comes to literature I am less malleable. Where the visual arts are concerned, I know myself to be a dunce; to music, I am tone-deaf; but I still think I know what I mean by vivid prose, I still prefer to read poetry for myself, instead of hearing it declaimed by an author who explains how good it is. Yet the current of contemporary thought erodes your judgment. Am I quite so sure of Keats as I was? Would a modern apprentice be encouraged to play the sedulous ape to Hawthorne? But there is worse; corrosion as well as erosion affects our literary loyalties; the mere lapse of time, the slowing down of life's pulses, can breed infidelity. I do not mean simply that we outgrow our calf love for this author or that; a Pater or a Swinburne. I mean that the masterpieces we still admire no longer have the power to thrill us; use has staled them, and our worship, however sincere, has grown mechanical. We acknowledge their merit, we recommend them to others, but for ourselves the charm has vanished; perhaps years hence, perhaps never to be recaptured. Dare I say it? I had this disillusionment, not long since, over *My Lady Nicotine*. For a lover of Barrie, and for one who re-reads more energetically than he reads, it was a depressing experience.

Amid all these devaluations in the currency of a man's taste, one or two favourite books survived, as possessing—what shall I say? I had almost called it "sterling worth"; but alas, the metaphor is no longer applicable as possessing an absolute quality, not depending for its appeal on the period at which each was written, nor on the period of life at which you read it; neither objectively nor subjectively is it dated. And, among the authors of such books, what a high rank belongs to Stevenson! No doubt, people's tastes differ, though like most people I am reluctant to admit that mine do. Still, assuming that a man enjoys normal mental health, is it not to be anticipated that he will count at least seven Stevensons on his list of the perennially re-readable? Certainly if he has not gone back to *The Wrecker* for the last ten years, he may be invited to shew cause for the omission.

Having laid down that broad principle, undeniable, I hope, within these four walls, I am tempted to go on and speculate why it is that Stevenson enjoys this effortless immortality. I do so with some hesitation, because the Club has kindly invited my brother-in-law to be one of its guests. And it seems to be the office of a brother-in-law—I have only one—to be forever asking questions; trying to pin you down to a considered opinion on this point or that, with the invariable rubric, "Would you say . . .?" The last thing in the world a man wants to have about when he is engaged in airy post-prandial speculations, excogitated *ad hoc*, about what constitutes a good author, and why one should read books one has read before. But I will take the risk. At the beginning of "Talk and Talkers" you will find a quotation from Benjamin Franklin: "As we must account for every idle word, so we must for every idle silence." On the latter count, we may take it for certain that Franklin had little to answer for; my own conscience is less easy.

First, then, I would say that Stevenson stays the course because he always takes the trouble to write well. Here, at once, I shall get into trouble with the moderns; what has writing well got to do with producing best-sellers? Writing well is a thing you do in Bloomsbury, on crinkly paper, for your friends who will review it. Novels should be stark, full of dots and dashes and italics, calculated to spread alarm and despondency; they pride themselves, do the novelists, on writing anyhow. Not all of them; Evelyn Waugh writes well; but it is not the habit of our time. But for Stevenson writing was not merely putting down marks on a piece of paper, to arouse impressions in the mind. He was a man who delighted in the sound of speech, and the written word was but the score of a musical composition; there must be no sentence which was not worthy of being read aloud. Prose was not, any more than verse, merely a question of balancing your sentences right, of selecting the precise word that did justice to your meaning, of avoiding the clumsy and the cacophonous. It had its own moods and cadences; the old distinction between prose as saying the right thing in the right way and poetry as saying the best thing in the best way was a blunder. There was a best way of saying anything, in prose as in poetry.

This conscientiousness may be a bad friend to a man's reputation; easy to mistake preciosity of phrase for deficiency of thought. It was in that sense, I suppose, that a particularly odious undergraduate at Oxford once said to me, the trouble about Stevenson was that he cared less about what he said than about the way he said it. A monstrous criticism, but you see what he meant. (Abbot Hunter-Blair had an uncle whose favourite conversational opening was "I see what yer mean, but yer wrong.") When I was at school, I was bracketed first for a prize poem, and Arthur Benson, who was examining, told me afterwards to go on writing poetry; it was a good way, he said, of learning how to write prose. Most of his readers would say that Arthur Benson would have written better prose if he had not been a poet. Stevenson, both in prose and verse, was the most conscious of artists. And, if I may risk a single controversial statement, I would suggest that he will rank higher, in the end, as a story-writer than as an essayist. As a story-writer, how he grips you in the telling! Not, indeed, that you must necessarily have style if you are to be re-readable. Trollope—no, I am not being modern; I knew him in and out before the moderns ever discovered him—Trollope is re-readable, and never was an author so content with utility English. But what a gracious accompaniment of the story, when it marches to music! "There was a thinning on the top of Pitman's head, there were silver hairs at Pitman's temples;

poor gentleman, he was no longer young, and years, and poverty, and humble ambition thwarted, make a cheerless lot" —do not tell me it would have made no difference to the story if that idea had been expressed just anyhow.

A second point which distinguishes Stevenson from the moderns; a second motive for going on reading him, although the hand which protrudes from the bed-clothes is beginning to experience the chill of these winter nights—he always has a story to tell you. In the old days, before the 1914 war, if you bought a novel you expected it to have a plot; the interplay of various human actions would lead up to a situation, a *dénouement*, breathlessly awaited, artistically inevitable. If it didn't, you demanded your money back—4*s.* 6*d.* over the counter or 6*s.* on your bill. Then the novelists found out— Monty Mackenzie and Hugh Walpole were in on the ground floor—that you could fool the public by giving it a novel which hadn't got a plot at all. A long slab of imaginary biography, diversified here and there with incidents, would do just as well. And you could boast that you despised novels with plots in them; just as people who can't afford to keep a gardener let their beds all go to grass nowadays, and pretend that they prefer it that way. Consider this piece of literary fact. When Evelyn Waugh joined the Commandos, he had written about a third of a book, two long chapters out of six or seven. It was to be an exciting book, almost a detective story, but he hadn't got on to that part. He published it, giving it the ingenious title of *Work Suspended*, and it was bought eagerly. People didn't notice that there was no ending—indeed that it hardly began; they just said "Here you have Mr. Waugh at his best". Consider that piece of literary fact, and then ask yourself what you would have given to see *Weir of Hermiston* finished.

Since I have taken it upon me to insult all the prejudices of this age in which we are condemned to linger, give me leave to complete the offence. The third reason which explains the charm, as it contributes to the greatness, of Robert Louis Stevenson is this; he was passionately interested in good and evil. I do not say, in right and wrong; anybody can be interested in right and wrong. But all his characters are moral agents; he regretted his inability, as an author, to endow them with free will. You can see that in one of his fables, "The Persons of the Tale", he calls it; Long John Silver, you will remember, and Captain Smollett, are discussing whether it was the author's choice one of them should, and the other should not, be a villain. I am not commenting on it as a contribution to theology; I am only pointing out how instinctively his own stories, even *Treasure Island*, appeared to Stevenson as arenas of moral conflict. The characters, for him, are not what they are for the moderns, a set of pathological specimens; they are centres of personal responsibility. And always they are a delicate compound of virtues and vices; how endearing are the very faults of his heroes, the vanity of Alan Breck, the commercial morality of Pinkerton! What a patchwork of qualities is Attwater, and how hard the reader must struggle to withhold his sympathies from the Master of Ballantrae! A villain you must have now and again for the sake of the plot, Alain or Uncle Ebenezer, but nobody is unrelieved black except Mr. Hyde. And he is black *ex hypothesi*; indeed, it is an excellent example of *exceptio probat regulam* that Stevenson could only conceive absolute malice as the result of a laboratory process. How engaging his tipplers are, Dr. Desprez, and Colonel Gordon in *Prince Otto*! Upon my word, I have a sneaking affection for the Admiral.

Because he saw through our virtues, Stevenson was a realist. Because he could make allowance for our vices, Stevenson was an optimist. He has some hard things to say about religion; the fable of the yellow paint hits home, and I am not sure that Captain Davis was ever really converted. But to one man at least, who was facing a young man's problems in the early nineties, it was Stevenson's influence—he had put it on record himself—that tipped the scale between optimism and pessimism. And it is something to have made an optimist of G. K. Chesterton.

We all remember Stevenson's essay on his grandfather; "I often wonder", he says, "what I have inherited from this old minister. I must suppose, indeed, that he was fond of preaching sermons; and so am I." Gentlemen, you have taken great risks by inviting here as your guest one who can boast of a clerical grandfather on both sides. You are in for a sermon, but you shall have it in brief. Is it fanciful to speculate that Stevenson inherited something also from his father, that was a builder of light-houses? By my way of it, he was a beacon, one of that chain of beacons across history that perpetuates the courage of mankind. Himself, he would have told you otherwise; his faith was too poor a thing, only the glimmer of a glow-worm's lamp. I do not know; but, such as it was, men saw the cresset, and the word was passed on.

Gentlemen, I have to thank you for your kindness in asking me to join you, for your patience in listening to me. I do not know whether it is a part of my duties to wish long life to the Club. But if so, let me do it in this formula, may the Club flourish, as long as Stevenson's works are known and loved on both sides of the Border! I could give you no fairer presage of perpetuity.

G. K. CHESTERTON

WHEN I undertook to give a lecture about G. K. Chesterton I felt, from the start, that the difficulty would lie not in finding material for it, but rather in cutting down the limits of my subject. As I thought it over, I felt more and more like the Oxford don, a Scot, I need hardly say, who undertook to write an essay for the Aristotelian Society on Induction; then wrote to the Secretary to say that after all his paper would be about the use of the Greek verb *epagein*; and then wrote again to the Secretary to say that his paper would be about the use of the verb *epagein* in Homer. On which subject he read for two hours continuously, and then explained that he would have to defer the second half of what he had to say until the next meeting. How was I to say little enough about Chesterton? I did not intend in any case to attempt any account of his life, and I am glad I did not. For, within the last week or two, the first instalments of his autobiography have begun to appear in the *Tablet*; a paper which I hope you all read. The instalments which have appeared have already disclosed things about Chesterton which I never knew, and perhaps I may add would never have guessed; as for example that his second name was Keith because his grandmother was a Scot. I never knew that; I didn't know it when I came to this city to support Chesterton's candidature, years ago, for the Lord Rectorship, and had flour emptied over me from the balcony of the Union Society's hall. I am not attempting to discuss that, or any other characteristic of Chesterton as a man. I am only going to discuss his works, and only a few out of the seventy or more books which he published. I decided to call my lecture "Chesterton in his Earlier Romances"; and with that limited treatment I am afraid my audience will have to be content.

It was a favourite principle of Chesterton's that it is possible to see a thing again and again, until it has become utterly staled to you by familiarity, and then suddenly to see it for the first time. Auberon Quin in *The Napoleon of Notting Hill*, walking behind two friends in frock coats, sees them all at once as two dragons, the buttons at the back of their coats being the eyes of the monster, and the slit its nose; two dragons walking away from him. And this faculty, he held, did not apply only to mere imaginaries; it was possible to have a vision of the truth in the same way; to see a thing as it really is for the first time, because all your nine hundred and ninety-nine previous glimpses of it had given you a merely conventional picture of it, and missed its essential truth. That is the burden of his introduction to *The Everlasting Man*; he outlines for us the picture of a primitive monster with a "strangely small head set on a neck not only longer but larger than itself", with "one disproportionate crest of hair running along the ridge of that heavy neck like a beard in the wrong place", with "feet, each like a solid horn, alone amid the feet of so many cattle"; and then it occurs to us that he is talking about the horse—only he is trying to make us see a horse as it really is for the first time in our lives, dwelling on its peculiarities instead of taking them for granted. He goes on to explain that it would do many of his contemporaries a lot of good if they could see for the first time, in this same way, a monster stranger even than the horse; the monster called Man.

For one at my time of life, brought up under the influences proper to that time of life, to write an article about Chesterton is to labour under precisely the same handicap. You are too familiar with the subject to be able to form any clear ideas about it. To me Chesterton's philosophy, in the broadest sense of that word, has been part of the air I breathed, ever since the age when a man's ideas begin to disentangle themselves from his education. His paradoxes have become, as it were, the platitudes of my thought. And this was a man whose genius touched everything; he had the universal grasp of his hero, Samuel Johnson, in days when literature had become at once more multitudinous and more specialized. He wrote of anthropology, archaeology, history ancient and recent, politics national and Continental, prose, poetry, theology, philosophy, art, criticism, what you will; they were the farrago of all his books; and in each department he appears, not as the competent journalist who has a knack of saying something about everything—though "journalist" was a title he rather welcomed than despised—but as a man of organic culture, who could really absorb what he read and digest it into his own system of thought. If a man proclaims himself a Marxian, he has given you a line on his political and economic beliefs; a Wesleyan, he has named his theological creed; a Freudian, you know something of his approach to the problems of the unconscious. If he should call himself a Chestertonian, you would see his whole attitude mapped out; it would include all the values of life. How is a man who has made Chesterton his hero any time these last thirty years to turn himself upside down and see Chesterton not as something taken for granted?

What I am trying to do here is to give some account, not of Chesterton as a man, but of his message. And in the main I am trying to interpret his message *as it reached me*, looking back on some half-dozen of his most self-expressive works as I read them when they first came out, and trying to remember what they meant to me. I do not mean that I shall follow an order of strict bibliography; but I shall have an eye, all the time, on the order in which his works came out. I do not know whether his message unfolded itself gradually to his own mind;

but, except perhaps among his close friends, it certainly did
so to the minds of his readers.

I was a school-boy, just beginning to think, when *The
Napoleon of Notting Hill* appeared. You have to read that book
(the first, I suppose, which really drew attention to him,
though his life of Browning came earlier) with the picture of
the Boer War as its background. You must attempt to imagine
—it is almost unimaginable in our day—the atmosphere of
Jingo imperialism in which the ordinary boy of the period had
been brought up. Criticism of that attitude, satire upon that
attitude, was already making itself felt; I think Belloc's
Emmanuel Burden, one of the greatest satirical works in our
language, came out in the same year as *The Napoleon*. But
Belloc wrote like an old man in his youth; just as Chesterton
wrote like a boy in late life. And in boyhood, although satire
may help to steady you, it is an ideal that you demand. *The
Napoleon of Notting Hill* presented, quite suddenly, to imperialist England the idea of a small nation as something desirable
for itself. You might start by regarding it as a joke, just as
Auberon Quin drew up the Charter of the Cities for a joke.
But there was a wand which could turn that comedy into
romance—the sword. Given a man who would take that joke
seriously, and it became necessary for a placid, effete, humani-
tarian imperialism to take the sword in its turn. The sense of
humour, product of an over-civilized mentality, must be
thrown to the winds; and that meant that Notting Hill had
won. Whatever its fortunes on the field of battle, it had won
in the field of ideas by making its opponents take it, and
themselves, seriously.

The book itself, like all Chesterton's work, was full of that
rhetorical form which we call paradox; it is probable that no
article or essay on paradox will ever be written in which
Chesterton is not mentioned, so much did he make the weapon
his own. But he made it his own in the spirit of King David,

smiting off Goliath's head with his own sword. Paradox, till then, had been regarded as a decadent device of the literary *flâneur*; it had enabled Oscar Wilde to tickle us with pleasant nonsense in *The Importance of Being Earnest*. Chesterton, setting out on his self-appointed task of massacring the decadents, began by wresting their own weapon from their hands. Or, at best, you thought of it as a convenient cloak under which Bernard Shaw would wrap up his more audacious sophistries, attacking our most sacred notions (that of the family, for example, in *You Never Can Tell*). Chesterton, setting out to defend these sacred notions, would begin by turning the stone which the builders rejected into the head of the corner. In an age which had gone mad over a hundred speculative fanaticisms, whose prophets had saturated the public with literary cleverness, it was not enough to state the case for sanity in plain terms. You must retort their own methods on the sophists, making truth appear something more dazzling, more daring, more original than error.

But it was not merely that the book contained paradoxes; the whole idea of the book *was* a paradox—to us. We had grown so accustomed to the idea that the happiest destiny which could fall to the lot of any nation was to be incorporated into the British Empire—and here was a man telling us that the small nation had a positive value of its own; that the infinite variety of a world divided up into small states, each with its own fierce loyalties, its own precious individuality, was an ideal which could be set over against our own unreflecting ideal of painting the map red. This was to be, in great part, Chesterton s message. But he did not confine the patronage of his genius to small nations; he extended it to small institutions—to the small landed proprietor who was being cleared off the scene to make room for scientific farming, to the small shop-keeper who was being frozen out by the big chain-stores, with their threat of "Amalgamate or starve".

That the joy of ownership, the right of a man to express himself in his work, instead of being a hired servant working to the orders of another, should be extended to the greatest possible number of citizens, was thenceforward an idea which dominated Chesterton's mind, and it is in large part the meaning of the political philosophy which he founded, what is known as Distributism.

Whether it is a practical ideal, or whether, human nature being what it is, and human opportunities being what they are, it is bound to remain an ideal only, is a question we have no time to discuss here. Certainly Chesterton himself was not blind to its difficulties; in the story, it will be remembered, Notting Hill has no sooner become an independent city than it begins to turn into an empire; the same patriotism which hitherto had made its story an epic of freedom inspired it to play the tyrant in its turn; so the wheel goes round. Just so Mr. Turnbull's shop, which was called a toy-shop but really sold almost everything else in the world, "tobacco, exercise books, sweet-stuff, novelettes, halfpenny paper-clips, halfpenny pencil sharpeners, bootlaces, and cheap fireworks", the kind of shop Chesterton loved, is after all a multiple store in germ; the more it flourishes, the more it will extend, the more it extends, the more will lose individuality and become a home of paid clerks; there, but for the grace of God, goes Gordon Selfridge.

The Napoleon of Notting Hill only indicates that difficulty without attempting a solution of it. The book concludes, instead, by opening up a wider problem; which was right, Quin who invented Notting Hill for a joke, or Wayne who did not see that it was a joke, and turned it into a reality? Which is right, the cynic who sees everything as amusing, or the fanatic who has no sense of humour at all? The answer to that is that the two men are in reality only two lobes of one brain; it is only when the world goes wrong that the pure precipitation of cynic or of fanatic is formed; the normal man, living in normal surroundings, is a blend of both. Laughter and love are everywhere; in healthy people there is no war between them. So Chesterton defended himself, once for all, against the world which would alternatively accuse him of being too flippant or of taking things too seriously. If he did either, it was their fault, not his. It was because the times had gone wrong.

The Napoleon of Notting Hill was followed up by *Heretics*, a *Syllabus Errorum* which defines and defies those tendencies in contemporary thought and literature from which Chesterton reacted; some of them will only be remembered because Chesterton reacted from them. I must pass it over, since I have determined to confine myself to the romances. But I think it is probable that, when he had published it, Chesterton began to feel more at peace with the world because he had said his say. He had cleared up his mind, and cleared it up in public, about the people he disagreed with and his reasons for disagreeing with them. His message might not have travelled far, but at least it had now achieved definition, though only a negative kind of definition. His next important romance—*The Club of Queer Trades* contains much excellent fantasy, but it would hardly rank as an important book—is *The Man who was Thursday*. It came out in 1908, when I was an undergraduate; and so rich is it in abrupt transitions from the flippant to the serious and back again that I always think of it as a young man's book, written by some contemporary of my own. As a matter of fact, Chesterton was thirty-four years of age, and the dedication of it, to his school friend Mr. Bentley, shews him already looking back on his extreme youth, as a time of somewhat exaggerated fears and unnecessarily anguished striving.

Science announced nonentity, and art admired decay;
The world was old and ended, but you and I were gay.

He recalls the struggle of the soul which it had cost, in the closing decade of last century, to keep faith or hope alive in an atmosphere, a literary atmosphere, of prevailing pessimism. He recalls the debt which he owed, and paid later on, to Robert Louis Stevenson, with his desperate attempt to be an optimist. The story is "a tale of those old fears, even of those emptied hells"; there is a sense of relief, though not of victory, in every line of it. It is not that the world has yet returned to sanity; still less that Chesterton has capitulated at any point to its insanities. But he can take a clearer, calmer view now of the forces against which he has contended, and is still contending; it is in that spirit that the story itself is written.

The story is a fantasia, perhaps unique in literature; I have described it elsewhere as something akin to rewriting the *Pilgrim's Progress* in the style of the Pickwick Papers. You can read it, up to the beginning of the last chapter, as a mere adventure story; that of the police agent who enrols himself as an anarchist, to discover gradually that the other members of the supreme council, all except the President, are in the same position as himself. He thinks at one moment that the whole world has gone anarchist, when he finds himself with four of the police, his companions, pursued by an angry mob over the countryside; only to discover that the mob are behaving in that way because they are mistaking the police for anarchists. But in the last chapter, where the President of the Anarchist Council turns out to be the Man in the dark room, the Chief of Secret Police who issued to them their commission to fight against anarchy, they demand explanations; and the explanations cut deep into philosophy; nay, into theology. "Why does each small thing in the world have to fight against the world itself? . . . For the same reason that I had to be alone in the dreadful Council of the Days. So that each thing that obeys law may have the glory and isolation of the anarchist. So that each man fighting for order may be as good and brave as the dynamiter. . . . No agonies can be too great to buy the right to say to this accuser, We also have suffered.''

I may be entirely wrong, but I hazard the guess that the moral of *The Man who was Thursday* reflects a moment in Chesterton's life when his religious beliefs had taken clear shape; when he had "made his soul". It was in the same year, 1908, that he produced *Orthodoxy*, a book which should certainly have been followed by his immediate reception into the Church, if the gift of faith itself always came with that orientation of the mind which is its natural counterpart. It is only guess-work, but I think that must have been the moment at which Chesterton really began to feel certain of himself, and therefore began to show more tolerance towards others. Perhaps, in age, he had reached that "shock of maturity" of which Mr. Belloc writes; "the moment when a man is grown up, when he sees things as they are, that is, backwards, and feels solidly himself". Anyhow, I suppose the philosophical moral of *The Man who was Thursday* is that the people we fight against because we see them to be in the wrong are, after all, fighting for some distorted vision of the right; each has the policeman's card in his pocket, and thinks you an anarchist as surely as you think him one.

Did that mean to say that, after all, one cause is as good as another as long as you fight manfully for it, and have the experience, as Stevenson would say, of "thrilling with the joy of girded men" while you do so? That what matters is not the cause for which we work, but the spirit in which we work for it? If anybody hoped, for a short while, that Chesterton would accept so monstrously un-Chestertonian a conclusion, the appearance, two years later, of *The Ball and the Cross* was admirably calculated to undeceive him. It came out about the same time as *What's Wrong with the World*, that telling collection of short articles in which Chesterton's political beliefs are stated and defended as his religious beliefs had been stated and defended in *Orthodoxy*. But *The Ball and the Cross*—I have an impression that the idea of it was roughed out some years earlier—confines itself to the theological sphere, and is undisguisedly a defence of controversy. It is the story of a Catholic Highlander and an atheist bookseller who determine to fight a duel in defence of their respective beliefs; their wanderings and escapes from the police and from other well-meaning persons who always manage to interrupt the duel when it seems to be just coming off, and how finally they are entrapped by two mad doctors, mad doctors in every sense, in an asylum where they meet all the sane people they have encountered in the course of the book, all as patients.

Now, it is true that this book is a glorification of fighting, that is, of controversy. It is true that the author admires the atheist printer, Turnbull, almost as much as MacIan, the hero, and puts into his mouth the most specious arguments available in favour of his unbeliefs—though still taking care, like Dr. Johnson, not to let "the Whig dogs have the best of it". But if you suggest that it does not really matter whether there be a God or no, so long as believers and atheists go on quarrelling honestly and spiritedly about the question of his existence—then you are falling into the precise error made in the book by the ex-don, Mr. Maurice Wimpey, who encouraged the two combatants to fight their duel in his garden, because he worshipped force and wanted to see a man die. They chased him into a scummy pond, at the sword's point; they would not leave him under his illusion that the sword's point was the point of swords. They fought, not for the joy of fighting, but to prove in the face of an indifferent world that the question over which they differed was worth fighting over; that the wars of religion were the only really just wars, the only really humane wars. That ultimate debate between God and materialism, which never left Chesterton's mind all through the thirty-five years of his literary activity, was a better thing to come to blows over than the possession of a few diamond mines. The true sanity is not that of the two mad doctors, who shut you up in an asylum if you quarrel over God's existence, because after all there is so much to be said for and against. The true sanity realizes that the truth, let it be what it may, matters furiously.

The Ball and the Cross introduces into Chesterton's romance a feature which was entirely absent in *The Napoleon of Notting Hill*, absent from all but half a dozen pages of *The Man who was Thursday*. It has a heroine; indeed, two heroines. Here is a point which is perhaps worth mentioning; in all Chesterton's stories you are never introduced to a woman he wants you to dislike. There is one fussy old lady in *Manalive*; there are one or two dangerous beauties in the Father Brown stories. But I do not think there is any author, with a literary output comparable to Chesterton's, who displays so consistently chivalrous an attitude towards the other sex. That is a digression, but I think it is worth making; it is of a piece with Chesterton's enormous reverence for women, with his knightly devotion, I do not know by what other name to call it, to the holy Mother of God.

The form of the three romances I have been discussing is always the same in outline; each is a dream ending in a nightmare. Chesterton wrote in an age when the apocalyptic type of romance was popular; the age of H. G. Wells in his prime, of Robert Hugh Benson, of the now forgotten Guy Thorne. But it was a treatment akin to his own genius; the broad sweep of his imaginative vision found its proper outlet in describing the last fatal battle in which the empire of Notting Hill went under; or the strange pageant in which the six policemen, dressed in flowing robes to personify the six days of Creation, make their complaint before the mysterious Master they have served; or the burning down of the madhouse, with the escape of nearly all, but not quite all, its inmates. He returned to it again, a little later, in *The Flying Inn*. But his next story, *Manalive*, though the spirit of the high wind that blows through its pages gives it something of a dream-like consistency, has nothing of this apocalyptic character; contains no situation of world-catastrophe. Nevertheless, it is an allegory. The figure of Innocent Smith is unmistakeably a type.

I have always wondered whether *Manalive* was modelled at all on Jerome K. Jerome's play, produced a few years before, *The Passing of the Third Floor Back*. There is a strong resemblance between the two; in either case a mysterious stranger arrives suddenly at a London boarding-house, and although he only stays there a few days, leaves all the various characters in it the better for his visit. If Chesterton really had reminiscences, even unconscious, of Jerome's play in his mind, the twist he has given to the situation in his treatment of it is at once startling and characteristic. Jerome's mysterious stranger was played by Forbes Robertson, enveloped in a great cloak and talking in impressive tones as if to guarantee a supernatural origin. The mysterious stranger of *Manalive*, if he is modelled on anybody, must have been modelled on the old gentleman in *Nicholas Nickleby*. He puts everybody in a good temper, though they regard him as a harmless lunatic. But when he shoots holes in the hat of a visiting psychologist, and when a long dossier is produced which purports to identify him as a murderer and a housebreaker who has deserted his wife and eloped several times with women who were never heard of again, the harmlessness of his lunacy is called in doubt, and a kind of judicial investigation is conducted by the boarding-house guests.

It proves, of course, that the eccentric, Innocent Smith, is a crack shot who threatens pessimists with a revolver till he makes them admit they are in love with life; an acrobat who climbs over roofs and breaks into his own flat, so as to sit in his own chair and drink his own port with a spice of adventure added to them; an energetic traveller who has been round the world for the sole purpose of coming back to his home as if it were some remote spot on a distant continent; a restless but singularly faithful husband who boards out his wife in odd places, and experiences, with never-failing zest, the thrill of eloping with her.

If you had asked Chesterton what he meant Innocent Smith to represent, I think he would have said, the innocence and the fresh eyes of childhood, investing with excitement and colour the drab surroundings—or so they have seemed hitherto —of half a dozen unsuccessful and disillusioned people. "He was an astral baby", says one of the characters, "born of all four of us, he was only our own youth returned . . . Once or twice, by the mercy of God, we may feel the same thing, but the man we shall never see. In a spring garden before break-fast we shall smell the smell called Smith. In the snapping of brisk twigs in tiny fires we shall hear a noise called Smith", and so on; in fact he is a spirit, the spirit of youth re-born.

I do not think it ever occurred to Chesterton that he was, in a sense, writing an autobiographical novel. Yet in fact Chesterton was Innocent Smith, and his effect on the world was the effect Smith had on the boarding-house. Only Smith, like Professor Chadd in *The Club of Queer Trades*, would express by actions what Chesterton expressed by his words. Chesterton taught us that life was after all worth living, if only we would see its values from a new angle—as the Warden of Brakespeare did when he hung upside down from the gargoyle on the bridge. Chesterton was often accused of being a Socialist by people who heard him denouncing the great fortunes of the very rich, until they learned to recognize his devotion to the idea of ownership, as that is expressed in the lives of the moderately poor. Chesterton made us see the value of old institutions, the cogency of old truths, by dint of

travelling round the world, as it were, to rediscover them—
by re-interpreting truisms as the paradoxes they really were,
things staled by familiarity as the exciting, adventurous things
they really were. Chesterton made us see that romance lies,
not in flitting, out of boredom, from one amorous adventure
to another, but in experiencing, and returning, a life-long
fidelity.

It would seem natural to add here some considerations of
the last complete romance Chesterton brought out in his pre-
War period, I mean *The Flying Inn*. But, although it will always
be read, if only for the songs and poems with which it is inter-
spersed, it has not that unity of design which characterizes the
books we have been discussing hitherto. It leans much on
satire; and the satire has a variety of targets—Puritans, sham
philanthropists, food-faddists, politicians, Jews, Turks, infidels,
sentimentalists, decadence in literature and in art. It is as if
Chesterton had been trying to rewrite *Heretics* in the form of a
novel; there is no continuous thread of argument which binds
it together except the Chestertonian glorification of common
things—beer and donkeys and songs sung in the hour of peril,
and the homely courage and honesty of the poor. The truth
is, I think, that by now Chesterton was writing so much, and
in so many different media, that his attack on the heresies of
his day was no longer concentrated in a few hammer-blows as
heretofore. This period just before the War is the period of
Magic, *The Ballad of the White Horse*, the *Innocence* and then the
Wisdom of Father Brown, *George Bernard Shaw*, *The Victorian Age
in Literature*, besides what he contributed to *The Eye-Witness*
(later *G. K.'s Weekly*), and his regular articles in *The Illustrated
London News*. I do not think it was true of Chesterton, at any
time of his life, that he wrote too much; he may have en-
dangered his health, but he did not endanger his style or the
quality of his output; the fertility of his genius seemed inexhaustible. But he was concentrating less on the output of

allegorical fiction; and to trace the further development of his ideas would need a much fuller treatment than I have room to give it here.

It is probably true that Chesterton's earlier work was more influential than his later work, at any rate in the department of fiction. The figure of Father Brown, once it was invented, leaped into favour with the fiction-reading public; he was so obviously the most successful of a hundred attempts to create a detective who should not be like Sherlock Holmes. And that public—it is a weakness with any sort of public—demands that a success should be indefinitely repeated; The Man who Knew too Much might be a sort of detective, and the stories of the Four Faultless Felons might be mystery stories; but where was Father Brown? He was almost too successful a creation; he was in danger of swallowing up his author. The Father Brown stories have had, I should suppose, an enormous sale, the earlier ones especially. And they are full of Chesterton, as everything that Chesterton ever wrote was full of Chesterton. But I would not say they have been influential with the generation that has grown up since 1918, as The Napoleon of Notting Hill and The Man who was Thursday were influential with ours. Partly because the message Chesterton preached was by now less of a surprise; you took it for granted instead of meditating upon it. Partly because the Father Brown stories are so good merely as detective stories, that it is possible to overlook the moral in most of them in your appreciation of their literary excellence—you are tempted, sometimes, to skip over the moral in your impatience to reach the explanation of the mystery.

You were not meant to do that. Nearly always, there is a philosophical or at least a political idea at the very heart of each story. If Chesterton based one of his mysteries on the simple and familiar fact that a waiter is dressed like a diner, he did not mean you to stand aghast at the genius which could create a puzzle out of it. He meant you to reflect on the singular character of a civilization which can make a diner so very much like a waiter, and at the same time so very different. If he described a postman as an invisible man, a mentally invisible man, because you so take him for granted that you say nobody has entered a house when in fact you have seen a postman enter a house, he meant you to realize where bureaucracy is leading us. If Professor Openshaw, the authority on psychic occurrences, fails to see through the very incomplete disguise adopted by his secretary, because, although he has given the man his orders for years, he has never really looked at him, what we are called upon to exclaim at is not so much the ingenuity of the secretary as the inhumanity of Professor Openshaw. I think I am right in saying that in practically every Father Brown story the mystery depends, not on some *material* possibility which we have overlooked (as in the case of the man who was stabbed with an icicle in the Turkish bath, or the medicine bottle which was not shaken up to counteract the poison, or the swamp adder that was let in by the skylight, and so on), but on some kink of human thought, some trick of human behaviour, which is worth a sermon to the little priest who sees through the difficulty, and knows humanity because of, not in spite of, his knowledge of divinity. But how many of Father Brown's admirers really stop to listen to the sermon?

Will Chesterton be remembered; and if so, will he be remembered as a writer of romances? That he himself should be speedily forgotten, is the prayer of every true prophet. He sees the world at fault, and fulminates accordingly; he would be only too glad that soon after his death, if not in his own life-time, the world should have so thoroughly corrected its faults as to make the fulminations seem unnecessary, fantastic, echoes of a dead world, possessing a merely period interest. So Michael, the Bulgarian recluse in *The Ball and the Cross*, has spent his time in constructing really admirable refutations of "certain heresies, the last professors of which had been burnt, generally by each other, precisely 1,119 years previously". Chesterton, where he is now, could hear no better news than that his own book *Heretics* was similarly out of date. There is perhaps more danger that he should be forgotten for the opposite reasons. It may be that the tendencies against which he fought, mass-production, industrial slavery, sentimental evasion of moral principles, senseless curtailment of human liberties, and so on, will come to be more and more with us, till the world finds it incredible that such protests as his were ever made. Most probably, I think, he will be remembered as a great imaginative artist, whatever course the world takes. And by us Catholics, who have a long memory, not only for the saints, he will certainly be remembered as a man who fought always on the side of the angels, a great model, to the authors of all time, of two virtues in particular, innocence and humility. And if the world remembers him only by his more polished productions, *The Ballad of the White Horse*, for example, and some of his biographies, and *The Everlasting Man*, Catholic boyhood will still, I think, be brought up on those thrilling earlier romances of his, on the battle fought in the dark about the streets of Notting Hill, and the anarchist chasing the police through the French countryside, and the President of Brakespeare College being forced, at the revolver's point, to thank God for the ducks on the pond. I at least hope so; for with these memories goes my own youth.

FATHER BROWN

WHEN you met Chesterton in life, the physical bigness of the man made him seem out of scale; he overflowed his surroundings. And the same thing is true, in a curious way, of his literary output; he never really found his medium, because every medium he tried—and how many he tried!—was too small a receptacle for the amount of himself he put into it. He stood alone in the remarkable generation to which he belonged in being perfectly integrated; he had a philosophy of life, and not of this life only, which was all of a piece, and it so possessed him that he could not achieve, in any particular form of writing, mere literary perfection. His life of Dickens is an admirable performance, but it is really the Chestertonian philosophy as illustrated by the life of Dickens; his *History of England* is a brilliant *résumé*, but it is a history of Chesterton rather than of England. Shaw kept on urging him to write plays, but when *Magic* was produced it was too good for the stage; an after-dinner audience was not capable of the intellectual effort demanded of it. Even *The Ballad of the White Horse*, one of his certainly immortal works, cannot be graded among English epics because it is so much more than an epic. And the same fate pursued him in that fortunate moment when he took to writing detective stories. When we founded the Detection Club, he was appointed, without a dissentient voice, as its first president; who else could have presided over Bentley and Dorothy Sayers and Agatha Christie and those others? Yet the Father Brown stories cannot really be graded among mystery stories; they are mystery stories with a difference. As usual, the box has been so tightly packed that the clasps will not fasten; there is too much meat in the sandwich.

When you take to writing detective stories, the measure of your success depends on the amount of personality you can build up round your favourite detective. Why this should be so, is not immediately obvious; it might have been supposed that this kind of fiction had a merely mathematical appeal. But, whether because Sherlock Holmes has set the standard for all time, or because the public does not like to see plots unravelled by a mere thinking-machine, it is personality that counts. You are not bound to make your public *like* the Great Detective; many readers have found Lord Peter Wimsey too much of a good thing, and I have even heard of people who were unable to appreciate the flavours of Poirot. But he must be real; he must have idiosyncrasies, eccentricities; even if he is a professional policeman, like Hanaud, he must smoke those appalling cigarettes, and get his English idioms wrong. And if possible—perhaps that is where Lord Peter fails—he must appeal to us through weakness; when he appears on the scene of the tragedy, the general reaction must be "A man like that will never be able to get at the truth." It is because he drops his parcels and cannot roll his umbrella, because he blinks at us and has fits of absent-mindedness, that Father Brown is such a good publisher's detective. He is a Daniel come to judgment.

He was "based", as we say, on Monsignor John O'Connor of Bradford; it was he who later received Chesterton into the Church. The occasion on which Father Brown came into being is well documented, both in Chesterton's autobiography and in Monsignor O'Connor's memoir of him; and it should serve for a specimen of what is meant when we are told that such and such a character in a book was "based" on such and such a figure in real life. Two young acquaintances of Chesterton's, having been introduced by him to this new clerical friend, expressed surprise afterwards that a man trained in the seminary should possess such knowledge of the world, especially of the criminal world. Chesterton was delighted with their *naïveté*; was it not to be expected (he said to himself) that a man who spent three hours every Saturday listening to the tale of other people's sins should have some acquaintance with the by-ways of human depravity? And this reflection was incorporated bodily in the first of the Father Brown stories, *The Blue Cross*:

> "How in Tartarus," cried Flambeau, "did you ever hear of the spiked bracelet?"
>
> "Oh, one's little flock, you know," said Father Brown.

That was all, really; nobody who had met Monsignor O'Connor would have put him down as "a clerical simpleton". He may have had difficulties about folding his umbrella; but instinctively you felt that this priest was a shrewd judge of men, with a reading of history and literature beyond the common. The owlish eyes blinking at you, the wooden indifference to appearances, the prosaic trudge in pursuit of his day-to-day tasks— all that was not Monsignor O'Connor as Chesterton saw him, but Father Brown as Chesterton invented him. He simply decided that for his own purposes—if I may put it in that way— he wanted a detective as unlike Lord Peter Wimsey as possible.

There was to be nothing of the expert about Father Brown; he should have no knowledge of obscure poisons, or of the time required to let the *rigor mortis* set in; he was not to be the author of any treatise about the different kinds of cigarette ashes. All his knowledge was of the human heart; he explains, in *The Secret of Flambeau*, that he is only capable of detecting murder mysteries because he was the murderer himself—only, as it were, *in petto*. "What I mean is that, when I tried to imagine the state of mind in which such a thing would be done, I always realized that I might have done it myself under certain mental conditions, and not under others; and not generally the obvious ones. And then, of course, I knew who really had done it; and he was not generally the obvious person.'' He could put himself inside the other man's skin. He could even put himself inside an animal's skin—no, the dog did not know the murderer by instinct and spring at him, that was sentimental mythology. The important thing about the dog was that it howled when the sword-stick was thrown into the sea—howled because the sword-stick didn't float.

The real secret of Father Brown is that there is nothing of the mystic about him. When he falls into a reverie—I had almost said, a brown study—the other people in the story think that he must be having an ecstasy, because he is a Catholic priest, and will proceed to solve the mystery by some kind of heaven-sent intuition. And the reader, if he is not careful, will get carried away by the same miscalculation; here, surely, is Chesterton preparing to shew the Protestants where they get off. Unconsciously, this adds to the feeling of suspense; you never imagine that Poirot will have an ecstasy, or that Albert Campion will receive enlightenment from the supernatural world. And all the time, Father Brown is doing just what Poirot does; he is using his little grey cells. He is noticing something which the reader hasn't noticed, and will kick himself later for not having noticed. The lawyer who asks ''Where was the body found?'' when he is told about the Admiral's drowning has given himself away as knowing too much, already, about the duck-pond; if he had been an honest man, he would have assumed that the Admiral was drowned at sea. The prophet who goes on chanting his litany from the balcony, when the crowd beneath is rushing to the aid of the murdered woman, gives himself away as the murderer; he was expecting it. We had all the data to go upon, only Father Brown saw the point and we didn't.

What is the right length for a mystery story? Anybody who

has tried to write one will tell you, I think, that it should be about a third of the length of a novel. Conan Doyle uses that formula in *A Study in Scarlet*, and in *The Valley of Fear*, filling up the rest of the book with a long story which does not really affect the plot. The modern publisher expects a full-length novel (which demands either a second murder or a great deal of padding), or else a short story (in which it is difficult for the author to give us the full conditions of the problem). Father Brown began life as short stories in the *Saturday Evening Post*, and short stories he remained; for an author so fertile in ideas, perhaps it was the simplest arrangement. But it must be confessed that this enforced brevity produces a rather breathless atmosphere; the more so, because Chesterton was an artist before he became an author, and occupies a good deal of his space with scene-painting. And the scene-painting takes up room—valuable room, the pedantic reader would tell us.

What scene-painting it is! The Norfolk Broads, and the house full of mirrors standing on its lonely island; or that other island on the Cornish estuary, with its wooden tower—you would expect the second of these pictures to be little more than a repetition of the first, but in fact it is nothing of the kind; in the one case you have the feeling of being in Norfolk, in the other you have the feeling of being in Cornwall. The atmosphere of that dreadful hotel in *The Queer Feet*; the atmosphere of a winter-bound summer resort in *The God of the Gongs*; the (quite irrelevant) effect of bitter cold in *The Sign of the Broken Sword*—what a setting they give to the story! Flambeau explains, at the beginning of *The Flying Stars*, that in his criminal days he was something of an artist; "I had always attempted to provide crimes suitable to the special seasons or landscapes in which I found myself, choosing this or that terrace or garden for a catastrophe"; and if the criminal, so limited in his choice of means, can be expected to provide a suitable *décor*, how much more the writer of stories! Yet it is only Chesterton who gives us these effects, the "topsy-turvydom of stone in mid-air" as two men look down from the tower of a Gothic church; the "seas beyond seas of pines, now all aslope one way under the wind" on the hill-side of Glengyle; the "green velvet pocket in the long, green, trailing garments of the hills" on to which Mr. Harrogate's coach overturns, ready for the coming of the brigands. Did Chesterton pick out these landscapes with his artist's eye, and then, like Flambeau, invent crimes to suit them?

But it does take up room. And, if only because the canvas is so overcrowded, you must not expect in these stories the mass of details which you would expect of Freeman Wills Crofts; the extracts from Bradshaw, the plan of the study with a cross to shew where the body was found. Hence the severely orthodox readers of detective stories, who love to check and to challenge every detail, must be prepared for a disappointment; Chesterton will not be at pains to tell us whether the windows were fastened; how many housemaids were kept (in defiance of modern probabilities), and which of them dusted the room last; whether a shot in the gun-room would be audible in the butler's pantry, and so on. Even the unities of time and place are neglected; you can never be quite sure whether it is next morning, or a week later, or what. Consequently, you never quite feel "Here am I, with all the same data at my disposal as Father Brown had; why is it that his little grey cells work, and mine don't?" Not that there is any deliberate concealment of clues, but the whole picture is blurred; the very wealth of detail confuses you. All you can do is to set about eliminating the impossible characters in the hope of finding, by a process of exhaustion, the villain. Women can be ruled out; there is only one female villain in the whole series—it is part of Chesterton's obstinate chivalry that he hardly ever introduces you to a woman you are meant to dislike. People with Irish names (how unlike Sherlock

Holmes!) are fairly certain to be innocent. But, even so, the characters of the story elude you; you do not feel certain that you have been told quite enough about them.

For Chesterton (as for Father Brown) the characters were the really important thing. The little priest could see, not as a psychologist, but as a moralist, into the dark places of the human heart; could guess, therefore, at what point envy, or fear, or resentment would pass the bounds of the normal, and the cords of convention would snap, so that a man was hurried into crime. Into crime, not necessarily into murder; the Father Brown stories are not bloodthirsty, as detective stories go; a full third of them deal neither with murder nor with attempted murder, which is an unusual average nowadays; most readers demand a corpse. The motives which made it necessary for Hypatia Hard to elope with her husband, the motives which induced the Master of the Mountain to pretend that he had stolen the ruby when he hadn't—the reader may find them unimpressive, because there is no black cap and no drop at the end of them. But, unless he is a man of unusual perspicacity, he will have to admit that he also found them unexpected.

The truth is that what we demand of a detective story is neither sensations, nor horrors, but ingenuity. And Chesterton was a man of limitless ingenuity. What really contents us is when we see at last, and kick ourselves for not having seen before, that the man who was murdered in the Turkish bath without any trace of a weapon was stabbed with an icicle; that the poisoner did drink the tea which accounted for her victim, but took a stiff emetic immediately afterwards; that the time of a particular incident was given wrongly, not because the witness was in bad faith, but because she saw, not the clock, but the reflection of the clock in a looking-glass. All those brilliant twists which a Mason and an Agatha Christie give to their stories, Chesterton, when he was in the mood for it, could give to his. How to dispose of the body? If it was only for a short time, you could hang it up on the hat-stand in a dark passage; if you wanted to get rid of it altogether, you could bury it in the concrete floor of a new set of flats. A ship could be lured to its doom by lighting a bonfire which would confuse the appearance of the lights in the tideway; you could gag a ruler so securely that he would be unable to answer the challenge of his own sentries, and would be shot. They are all ideas we might have thought of, and didn't.

Whether such expedients would be likely to be adopted in real life is perhaps more questionable. But then, how far is the writer of mystery stories bound by the laws of probability? Nothing could be more improbable than Father Brown's habit of always being on the spot when a crime is committed; but he shares this curious trick of ubiquity with Hercule Poirot. The thing is a literary convention; it may not be a good one, but it is well worn. No, when we open a detective story we leave the world of strict probability behind us; we must be prepared for three or four quite independent pieces of shady business happening to happen in the same country house on the same evening. And Chesterton's imagination was flamboyant; he was like a schoolboy on holiday, and could sit as light to realism as P. G. Wodehouse. If you meet him on his own ground—that is, halfway to fairyland—you will have to admit that for sheer ingenuity he can rival Miss Sayers herself. Cast your mind back to your first reading of the Father Brown stories, and ask yourself whether you saw what was the missing factor which linked all the various exhibits in Glengyle Castle, or why *The Insoluble Problem* was insoluble.

No, if we are to judge the Father Brown cycle by the canons of its own art, we shall not be disposed to complain that these are something less than detective stories; rather, that they are something more. Like everything else Chesterton wrote, they are a Chestertonian manifesto. And it may be reasonably maintained that a detective story is meant to be read in bed, by way of courting sleep; it ought not to make us think—or rather, it ought to be a kind of *catharsis*, taking our minds off the ethical, political, theological problems which exercise our waking hours by giving us artificial problems to solve instead. If this is so, have we not good reason to complain of an author who smuggles into our minds, under the disguise of a police mystery, the very solicitudes he was under contract to banish?

I am inclined to think that the complaint, for what it is worth, lies against a good many of the Father Brown stories, but not all, and perhaps not the best. Where the moral which Chesterton introduces is vital to the narrative, belongs to the very stuff of the problem, the author has a right, if he will, to mystify us on this higher level. In the over-civilized world we live in, there are certain anomalies which we take for granted; and he may be excused if he gently mocks at us for being unable, because we took them for granted, to read his riddle. There is something artificial in a convention which allows us to say that nobody has entered a house when in fact a postman has entered it, as if the postman, being a State official, were not a man. There is something top-heavy about a society in which a fellow guest is indistinguishable from a waiter if he cares to walk in a particular way. And there is something lacking in the scientific investigator who can be taken in when his own secretary disguises himself in a false beard, simply because he has sat opposite his secretary day after day without noticing what he looked like. But it must be confessed that in some of the stories, especially the later ones, the didactic purpose tends to overshadow, and even to crowd out, the detective interest: such stories as *The Arrow of Heaven*, and *The Chief Mourner of Marne*. If we read these with interest, it is not because they are good detective stories, but because they are good Chesterton. When he wrote *The Incredulity* and *The Secret (of Father Brown)*, Chesterton had perhaps rather written himself out, and publishers pressed him for copy faster than even he could supply it. At the end of his life, he seemed to get a second wind, and *The Scandal of Father Brown* contains some of his most ingenious plots. But how seldom does an author manage to spin out a formula indefinitely; how signally Conan Doyle failed to do it! But—those first six stories Chesterton contributed to the *Saturday Evening Post*! How could that level have been maintained?

DETECTIVE STORIES

I DO not intend to make any apology for my choice of a subject this evening. The responsibility for that choice rests with the Secretary. I warned him that if I came—and I eagerly offered him the alternative of my not coming—I should have to read a frivolous paper on a frivolous theme. He accepted that alternative; and my audience has been fairly warned, I suppose, what it was letting itself in for. There is nothing left now but to go through with it.

Not that, on mature thought, I can consent to regard detective stories as a frivolous subject. I would regard them, rather, as one half of modern fiction. When I say fiction, I do not include biographies, nor yet treatises on the habits and outlook of primitive man; I mean fiction as the term is ordinarily understood. What has happened, surely, is this. Right up to the time of the War, when you bought a novel—and in those days, you must remember, one did *buy* novels, because they only cost four and sixpence net—you expected it to contain two principal ingredients, character, and a plot. Just before the War—I think it was Mr. Compton Mackenzie and Hugh Walpole who began it—novels began to appear which had a great deal of character-drawing in them, but no plot whatever. There was a story, to be sure, but it was just a story which went on and on; there were no complications, no *dénouements*, no poetic justice, no *peripeteia*; you were simply reading a slice of imaginary life. Nature abhors a vacuum; and the supply of novels which were all character and no plot created a demand for novels which were all plot and no character. Hence the rise of the detective novel.

Or, if you insist on treating the subject more analytically, let us say that all imaginative literature is an escape from real life. We cultivate it, true enough, so as to be able to meet within the covers of a book people even more unpleasant than the people we meet in real life. For that, the modern novel gives us ample opportunities. Bored with our friends, we take refuge in its interminable pages; and when we have finished with the crowd of conceited and pig-headed neuropaths, mostly resident in Chelsea, who form the stock-in-trade of its characters, we turn back to our own circle with a sense of positive relief. But this, you see, is not at all the escape we demand. We demand, besides, an escape from the urgency of those innumerable problems which confront our civilization. We can only do that by escaping to problems still more baffling, which nevertheless have an answer; and these are supplied by the detective story. That is why so many great men—it is notorious—read detective stories, though often behind locked doors, or under false jackets. They are afraid of their high-brow friends; for detective stories still do not rank as literature; I have yet to hear of any that won the Nobel prize. But we read them, for all that; and if you meet a man who boasts that he does not think them interesting, you will nearly always find that he indulges in some lower form of compensation—probably he is a cross-word addict. These facts being notorious, let us not consider it a waste of time to discuss the detective story. It is, as I shall hope to shew in the course of this lecture, a highly specialized art-form, and deserves, as such, its own literature.

What exactly is a detective story? The title must not be applied indiscriminately to all romances in which a detective, whether professional or amateur, plays a leading part. You might write a novel the hero of which was a professional detective who did not get on with his wife, and therefore ran away with somebody else's in Chapter 58, as is the wont of heroes in modern novels. That would not be a detective story. A detective story must have as its main interest the unravelling of a mystery; a mystery whose elements are clearly presented to the reader at an early stage in the proceedings, and whose nature is such as to arouse curiosity, a curiosity which is gratified at the end of the book.

And here let us draw a very clear line of demarcation, once for all, between detective stories and shockers. Shockers, by which I mean the complete works of Wallace, together with those of Le Queux and Oppenheim, and a cloud of their imitators, are not in the true sense mystery stories at all; they do not arouse a human instinct of curiosity. Suppose I go into a night club, and a fascinating woman with green eyes drops her handkerchief near me in passing out; and, when I politely stoop to pick it up, she whispers to me: "For God's sake keep clear of 133 Cromwell Gardens; and if you are ever set upon by thugs on the stairs of the Lancaster Gate Tube station, remember to ask them for the counter-sign of the Pink Spot" —all that, which is the practically invariable opening of what I call shockers, does not genuinely excite curiosity. It is not a mystery; it is simply an obvious lie. People would not say that sort of thing to me, and I should not dream of taking the trouble to go all the way to Cromwell Gardens if they did. One knows at once that the woman is an adventuress; probably a quite innocent one who is being compelled by a threat of blackmail to subserve the purposes of villains; one knows that there is a gang of international crooks at work, determined to put an end to the peace of Europe by giving away English State secrets to an unknown foreign power. One cannot foresee precisely what meeting-place the gang has, whether it will be a secret vault under Madame Tussaud's, or a house-boat at Maidenhead, or what; but you have read it all beforehand, and what you are quite certain of is that the motives of the villains will be entirely inhuman, the actions of the hero and heroine rash to the verge of idiocy; that the complications of Chapters 2 to 10 will not be explained in Chapter 58, because by that time the reader will certainly have forgotten all about them, and probably the author as well. All this is not a detective story. Personally I do not even think it is an interesting kind of story. I remember arguing this point in a letter to a friend who had been guilty of a rather superior thriller; and his view (he is a Catholic) was that he liked a little improbability about his romances, just as he did about his religion. I told him that I liked my romances to be probable, however untrue, and my religion to be true, however improbable. But I must not enter into all that. My point here is that, whatever they are, thrillers are not, properly speaking, detective stories, or even mystery stories. How, then, are we going to define what a detective story is?

To put it quite simply, the essence of the detective story is that in it the action takes place before the story begins. Of course, it is well to have one or two chapters at the beginning introducing us to the principal characters and especially to the future corpse or corpses. It is one of the weaknesses of Free-man Wills Croft that he sometimes presents us, in his first two chapters, with the body of a total stranger; at once he has missed a chance of invoking our human sympathies; nor does it make the case any better to discover, as we usually do, at the end of the book, that it was really a totally different total stranger all the time. No, Chapter 1 and perhaps Chapter 2 ought to introduce us to the main characters; but with Chapter 3 or thereabouts the curtain must suddenly go up on a murder or at least a crime already committed, ripe for investigation by the famous detective. The real action of the book is now over. And here is one of the chief difficulties about writing detective stories—to keep the interest alive in spite of the fact that what remains of the plot is, strictly speaking, not action at all, but mere unravelling. There are various ways of solving the difficulty; Mr. A. E. W. Mason, who stands, of course, in the very front rank of detective writers, always manages to get his heroine spirited away by villains early in the story, and Hanaud is careful not to rescue her until she is on the very point of being bumped off. Conscientious detective fans will always have the feeling that this method is a doubtful expedient; for, if the interest of the story is thus kept at a breathless level of excitement, we are apt to forget what the original mystery was about; we are apt, again, so rapidly are we carried along, to miss through carelessness clues that might otherwise have led us to the true solution of the mystery. Roughly speaking, it may be laid down that in the true detective story the elements of horror and violence are already over before the detective appears on the scene; and the story derives its romantic excitement only from the danger of the criminal getting off scot free, or some innocent person being condemned in his place.

It will be seen, therefore, that the detective story differs essentially from every other type of fiction. For the interest of the ordinary romance centres in the question, "What will happen?"—except in the case of the modern sex novel, where the interest centres in the question "When will anything happen?" But the interest of the detective story centres in the question "What has happened?" It is a *hysteron proteron Homerikos*. Ordinary romance was invented, one would think, by a wearied historian, who, finding himself, like most historians, unable to give a true account of the past, and willing, unlike most historians, to confess his inability, sat down to write a kind of literature in which all his characters behaved exactly as he wanted them to, because they had no existence outside his own brain. Whereas one would have expected the first writer of detective fiction to have been a scientist, who, giving up the riddles of his own craft, which either defied explanation or alternatively opened out fresh vistas of problems demanding fresh explanations, determined to set himself a problem which he *could* solve, because he and no other was responsible for the inventing of it. Ordinary fiction appeals to the synthetic in our natures, detective fiction to the analytic. Ordinary fiction works forwards from the conditions of the plot to its consummation, detective fiction works backwards from its consummation to its conditions. Indeed, I am trying to think up a quite new sort of crook film; the crime will be enacted at Hollywood exactly as it took place; but it will be turned into a detective film when it is shewn by the simple expedient of shewing it backwards.

Now that we have decided what a detective story is, we can proceed to investigate the history of the art. And let us beware of every one who tries to do things the other way about; who gives you a long historical introduction first, and then, only then, pauses to reflect what it is that he is talking about. By that time he has usually started talking about something quite different. Nearly all dons adopt this preposterous method, and its use is largely to blame for the barrenness and misleadingness of their results. Let us always define our terms beforehand, like Christians, and then perhaps our historical investigations will have value—but I appear to digress.

Not, indeed, that in this instance the historical investigation has any value whatsoever. The plain fact is that detective fiction has no history up to about the year 1840. People will tell you that the germs of the thing are to be found in the book of Daniel; do not believe them. It is true that in that book Daniel exposes the fraud practised by the priests of Bel, who used to come in at night by a secret door and eat up the offerings which had been left lying in front of the statue; and he exposed it ingeniously, by strewing ashes about on the floor and pointing to the footmarks which they left. The same method, of course, is used by Sherlock Holmes in the Mystery of the Golden Pince-nez. But the point is that although Daniel may have invented the art of detection, he did not invent the detective *story*; the incident is described in its historical order, and there is no attempt whatever to mystify the reader or to keep him in suspense. No, if I were anxious to find literary antecedents for the detective story, I should go to quite a different class of literature—to the Greek drama; and more especially to the *Oedipus Tyrannus.*

I can see that you are all trying to look as if you pretended to remember what the *Oedipus Tyrannus* is about; so I will give you a short sketch of the play to illustrate my thesis. There is an influenza epidemic in Thebes. The king, Oedipus, who has come to the throne many years before by marrying the widow of the late monarch, recently killed in a chariot accident, has sent Creon to Delphi to find out why the epidemic was sent by the gods. Creon, who is as far as possible the Watson of the play, comes back and reports that the curse can only be averted if the murderer of the late king, Laius, is found and banished. Who is he? Nobody knows. This gets Oedipus where he lives—you see, Oedipus was the man who guessed the riddle of the Sphinx, and by way of keeping up his reputation, he feels it is up to him to solve this mystery; he represents, roughly, Scotland Yard, the official police. No means of tackling the problem seems to occur to him except pronouncing a long and elaborate curse against the murderer, in the style of the Jackdaw of Rheims. Creon, as Watson, has a happier inspiration. "I know a man," he says, "who will see his way through this business," and goes out to fetch Tiresias, the famous blind detective. Tiresias at first refuses to speak, and then quite suddenly, without shewing his working, declares that Oedipus is himself the murderer of Laius. Oedipus thinks, and says, that this is a plot of Creon's to rob him of his throne. His wife, Jocasta, tries to reassure him by explaining that the late king, according to the evidence of the only surviving bystander, was killed by robbers, robbers in the plural, at the meeting of three roads. This most unfortunately reminds Oedipus of an occasion, just before he came to Thebes, when he encountered at just such a place an old gentleman who insisted on driving on the wrong side of the road, with fatal results for the old gentleman. It begins to look as if the blind detective had been right; but some uncertainty is still felt in official circles, because the Delphian oracle had distinctly prophesied that Laius would be killed by his own son. A doddering old herdsman is brought in, and his evidence shews not only that Laius was killed by a single assailant, but that Oedipus himself was Laius' long-lost son. So Oedipus goes into banishment and they all live unhappily ever afterwards.

Aristotle maintains that the *Oedipus Tyrannus* is a perfect example of dramatic construction. It is not, of course, perfectly constructed as a detective story; it is an early model. But it *is* constructed as a detective story; the truth about the past gradually coming out, and revealing itself to the actors in the drama one by one according to their various grades of intelligence. The only draw-back is that if you come across an edition of the play it is always preceded by a publisher's blurb in indifferent Iambics, which gives away the plot. They did not know, then, how to write jackets. But in itself the play is a mystery story.

From Sophocles we pass on to Edgar Allan Poe, and to Gaboriau. The true detective story seems to have sprung into being independently in France and in America. To Poe belongs the distinction, probably unique, of having written up a real crime in America as if it were an imaginary crime in France, of having solved the mystery, and, as it subsequently proved, having solved it right. The trouble about him is his interminable disquisitions about the laws of evidence, which hold up the action badly. Gaboriau is an earlier edition of Freeman Wills Croft; he is painstaking, but too painstaking, and you have to follow the detective laboriously through every stage of his investigations, without being rewarded with anything very sensational at the end of it.

There is no clear evidence that Gaboriau took his idea from Poe, though he wrote his first detective story in '66, and Poe died in the forties. Nor do I know of any evidence that Wilkie Collins took the idea from Gaboriau; though the date of *The Moonstone* ('68) is only two years later than Gaboriau's first triumph. *The Moonstone* is the first really complete detective story, with all the cross-currents of suspicion, all the misleading efforts of the characters to solve the mystery for themselves, and the marked individuality of Sergeant Cuff. It was two years later that Dickens died, leaving unfinished the manuscript of *Edwin Drood*; and the numerous attempts which were made in the succeeding years to find a clue to the murderer in that story may well have paved the way for the appearance of the great, the decisive, the final stage in sleuth evolution. *A Study in Scarlet* appeared in 1887, and since that date other things have been published, but it was only the detective stories that mattered.

So much for history. And now, what are the rules governing the art of the detective story? Let us remember in the first place that these are rules; and you cannot afford to overlook them, because the detective story is a game. People try to write poetry without rhyme and novels without plots and prose without meaning and so on; they may be right or they may be wrong, but such liberties must not be taken in the field of which we are speaking. For every detective story is a game played between the author and the reader; the author has scored if he can reach the last chapter without letting the reader see how the crime was committed, although he has given him hints all through which ought theoretically to have let him work it out for himself. And there will be no triumph in doing that if the author has broken the rules.

There are nine main rules, which I laid down in a book which nobody read, as long ago as 1924. I will give them here with a slight commentary.

I. The criminal must be someone who has been mentioned in the first five chapters, but it must not be anyone whose thoughts the reader has been allowed to follow. The first half of this rule is often broken by the worst detective writers. What on earth is the use of a mysterious stranger, whose very existence has never been suspected hitherto, turning up in chapter eleven? The second half of the rule is three times almost infringed by Agatha Christie—in *The Man in the Brown Suit, The Murder of Roger Ackroyd*, and in *The Seven Dials*, which is bad; but I think in every case if you read through the story again, you will be inclined to let her off. You did not suspect the criminal, because he seemed to be a person through whose eyes you had looked, and shared with them their mystification; but really Mrs. Christie was not deceiving you, she was allowing you to deceive yourself. The same may be said of *Murder at the Villa Rose*. By the way, one of the tests of a good detective story is that you should be able to read it a second time and enjoy seeing how you were spoofed.

II. All supernatural agencies or preternatural agencies are ruled out as a matter of course. To solve a detective problem by such means would be like winning a race on the river by the use of a concealed motor engine. And here I venture to think there is a limitation about Chesterton's Father Brown stories. He nearly always tries to put us off the scent by suggesting that the crime must have been done by magic. And we know that he is too good a sportsman to fall back upon such a solution. Consequently, although we seldom guess the answer, we usually miss the thrill of having suspected the wrong man.

III. Not more than one secret room or passage is allowable. I would add, that a secret passage should not be brought in at all unless the action takes place in the kind of house where such devices might be expected; the only time I introduced one myself I was careful to say beforehand that the house had belonged to Catholics in penal times. I think Milne's secret passage in *The Red House Mystery* is an unfair one; if a modern house were so equipped—and it would be villainously expensive—all the countryside would be quite certain to know about it.

IV. No hitherto undiscovered poisons may be used, nor any appliance which will need a long scientific explanation at the end. Conan Doyle violates the major principle of this rule, as far as I remember, in one of the later and more obviously spurious Holmes stories. There may be undiscovered poisons with quite unexpected reactions on the human system, but they have not been discovered yet, and until they are they must not be utilized in fiction; it is not cricket. All the cases of Dr. Thorndyke, recorded by Austin Freeman, have the minor medical blemish; you have to go through a long science lecture at the end of the story in order to understand how clever the mystery was.

V. No Chinaman must figure in the story. This principle, I admit, is one merely derived from experience; I see no reason in the nature of things why the Chinaman should spoil a detective story. But as a matter of fact, if you are turning over the pages of an unknown romance on a bookstall, and come across some mention of the narrow, slit-like eyes of Chin Loo, avoid that story; it is bad. The only exception I know is *The Four Tragedies of Memworth*, by Lord Ernest Hamilton.

VI. No accident must ever help the detective, nor must he ever have an unaccountable intuition which proves to be right. That is perhaps rather too strongly stated; it is legitimate for the detective to have inspirations which he afterwards verifies, before he acts on them, by genuine detective work. And again, he will naturally have moments of clear vision, in which the bearings of the observations hitherto made will suddenly become clear to him. But he must not be allowed, for example, to look for the lost will in the works of the grandfather clock because an unaccountable instinct tells him that is the right place to look in. He must look there because he realizes that that is where he would have hidden it himself. I suspect a certain weakness in this direction about Mr. Bailey's detective, Mr. Fortune; it may be that he simply does not take the trouble to explain his working, but it seems to me that he goes a good deal by guess-work.

VII. The detective must not himself commit the crime. This rule may of course be suspended where the detective is introduced as such, not on the author's responsibility, but on the responsibility of one of the characters, who may have made a mistake of identity. I have even read a very bad story in which the coroner was in league with the criminal. That will not do; there must be limits to the area of our suspicion.

VIII. The detective must not light on any clues which he does not instantly produce for the inspection of the reader. Any writer can make a mystery by saying that at this point the great Picklock Holes suddenly bent down and took up from the ground an object which he refused to let me see; "Ha!" he said, while his face grew grave. The skill of the detective writer lies in being able to produce his clues, flourish them defiantly in our faces—"There, what do you make of that?" —and we make nothing. So Holmes, in *Silver Blaze*: " 'Let me call your attention to the curious incident of the dog in the night-time.' 'The dog did nothing at all in the night-time.' 'That was the curious incident,' said Sherlock Holmes.'' Few readers really spot that the man who took the horse out was a man well known to the dog in the stables; yet none can complain that he was not given the chance of guessing.

IX. The stupid friend of the detective, the Watson, must not conceal from the reader any thoughts which pass through his mind. His intelligence must be slightly, but very slightly, below that of the average reader. This rule is only one of perfection; it is not of the *esse* of the detective story to have any Watson at all. But if he does exist, he exists for the purpose of letting the reader have a sparring partner, as it were, against whom he can pit his brains: "I may have been a fool," he says to himself as he lays the book aside, "but at least I wasn't such a doddering fool as old Watson."

These rules were not delivered to us by a revelation; they have been discovered, like most things in our experience, by a process of trial and error. Here, as in most other fields, you will find sentimentalists who commend the *naïf* simplicity of the earlier models. For myself, I should not really be inclined to award the palm to Conan Doyle. Let me apologize for the apparent irreverence of such a statement, and explain what I mean. I am not influenced, I think, by the fact that all his later efforts in this field were, to put criticism at its mildest, unworthy of his fame. He was in his literary dotage; it is a thing that may happen to any man; and the fact that a man cannot write a good story at the end of his life does not prove that he never could. No, greatly as I reverence the earlier stories of the Holmes cycle, I reverence them as old classics, models on which all later work in the same field has been based, and consequently never to be overthrown from their unique niche in literary history. The delineation of Holmes himself, in his best period, is of course irreplaceable; no subsequent detective of fiction has attained the same living personality. But the stories *as stories* have the simplicity of the old masters; and in detective fiction, or at any rate in the great game of reading detective fiction, simplicity will not do. I should like to get hold of a child, and supervise his education so carefully that his eye never lighted on a Holmes story until he had been put through a solid course of Christie, Bailey, and Cole; and then I should like to put Conan Doyle's work into his hands and see whether he could not guess all the mysteries at sight. I may be wrong, but I think he would emerge from the ordeal with credit.

Chesterton simply cannot be placed; he has no characteristic medium, but can make himself at home in any form of literary art, without obeying the rules of any. He is like some great hearty man who goes to the wickets without pads against county-cricket bowlers and hits them all over the field by unashamed slogging. *The Ballad of the White Horse* is not like any other poetry, nor *The Man who was Thursday* like any other romance, nor *Magic* like any other play, yet he succeeded beyond expectation in all of them. It happened one day (I am told) that Chesterton had no literary work on hand—it seems a strange thing to imagine—and wandered into the office of my literary agent—who was also his—to know if there was any publisher wanting anything done. The reply was "Nothing in your line, I am afraid, Mr. Chesterton; in fact the only thing we have heard of lately is the *Saturday Evening Post* wanting some detective stories." To which he replied, "Oh, well, I don't know," and, sitting down there and then in the office, wrote the first of the Father Brown stories. But are they detective stories? Is it possible to write an impressionist detective story? All one can say is that they are very good Chesterton.

It remains to say something about the future of the detective story. Let me admit at once that this seems rather dark. Nobody can have failed to notice that while the public demand remains unshaken, the faculty for writing a good detective story is rare, and the means of writing one with any symptom of originality about it becomes rarer with each succeeding year. The game is getting played out; before long, it is to be feared, all the possible combinations will have been worked out. Señor Capablanca appealed for brighter chess; he wanted a board with ninety-six squares, or something of that sort. But in what conceivable way are we to enlarge the possible horizons of this far more intriguing game, the solving of detective problems? We have seen how numerous and how stringent are the rules which necessarily govern its construction.

I say the detective story is in danger of getting played out. Even the exterior setting of the thing is by now almost stereotyped. We know, as we sit down to it, that a foul murder has almost certainly been done at a country house; that the butler will have been with the family for sixteen years; that a young male secretary will have been only recently engaged; that the chauffeur will have gone away for the night to visit his widowed mother. If life were like detective stories, we should all feel quite certain of getting jobs, so great would be the demand for young male secretaries; and it would be almost impossible for the father of a chauffeur to insure his life on any terms. We know that the murder—the public more or less demands a murder—will be done either behind the shrubbery in the grounds, or else in the dead man's study; if, however, the victim is a woman, she will be found dead in bed with an empty sleeping-draught bottle by her side. And so on.

But far more serious than this monotony of setting is the growing difficulty, for the author, in finding ways of deceiving his reader without either breaking the rules or using gambits which have been used *ad nauseam* before. I forget where it is that Bernard Shaw describes the growth of naval armaments as a senseless and unending competition between the theory of attack and the theory of defence. A. spends money on torpedoes, and B. has to spend money on torpedo-destroyers; A. invents a new form of mine, and B. has to lay down a new type of mine-sweeper. So it is with batting and bowling in cricket; so it is with serving and returning serves in lawn tennis; attack and defence improve alternately, each under the stress of competition with the other. And so it is with the great detective game; the stories get cleverer and cleverer, but the readers are getting cleverer and cleverer too; it is almost impossible at the moment to think up any form of bluff which the really seasoned reader will not see through.

Thus, in the old days, when a woman was found very uncomfortably bound to a chair, with her mouth gagged, and possibly only just recovering from the effects of an anaesthetic, we used to suppose, not unnaturally, that she had been tied up like that by the villains. Now we assume as a certainty that she is in league with the villains, and all the tying-up business was only fudge; we have so often had the old bluff worked off on us that it has ceased to take us in. Again, when the room is found covered with finger-marks or the lawn with foot-prints we know at once that these are false clues, arranged by the criminal so as to throw suspicion on an innocent person. That overdose of chloral has long ceased to mislead; there will be a half-empty bottle of it by the bedside, and the stomach of the deceased will be a mass of chloral, but we know for a dead certainty that the poison was administered somehow else—after death, as likely as not. The dead man found in the grounds was not murdered in the grounds; he was murdered miles away, and his corpse was brought there in a motor. The moment we come across any mention of a scape-grace brother who is supposed to have died in Canada, we know that he did not really die; but is going to reappear either as the villain or the victim, and will get mistaken for the original brother every time. The fact that there were signs of a struggle in the room always means that there was no struggle, and the furniture was deliberately thrown about afterwards; the fact that the window was left open is proof positive that the crime was committed from inside the house. All messages which come over the telephone are fake messages; people who are overheard telephoning in their rooms have never really taken the receiver off.

The possession of a good watertight alibi is perhaps the surest mark of the real criminal; the man who has wandered aimlessly about the streets of London for three and a half hours without meeting anyone who could swear to his identity is no less certainly innocent. Gone, too, are the old familiar tests by which, in the Victorian days, we used to know the good characters and the bad characters apart. Neither age nor sex is spared; the old country squire, who is a J.P. and has for years held his head high among his neighbours, so good, so kind, so charitable—watch him! The heroine, even, the friendless and penniless female who looks up with such appealing eyes into the face of the detective's friend, may quite possibly have done the fellow in; with a good deal of provocation, maybe, but handling the blunt instrument in no uncertain manner. The only person who is really scratch on morals is the aged butler; I do not recollect, off-hand, any lapse of virtue on the part of a man who has been with the family for sixteen years. But I may be wrong; I have not read *all* the detective stories.

It is possible that we shall get into a stage of double bluff, when the author will make his heroes look like heroes and his villains look like villains in the certainty that the reader will get it the wrong way round. Indeed, I did once myself write a story in which the curate was perfectly innocent and the dark, sinister man had committed the murder. I didn't mean it for a detective story; I hadn't written any detective stories then; I meant it for a satire on detective stories. It was rather a good satire, but the public insisted on taking it as a bad detective story. Anyhow, you couldn't play that game often; and you cannot go on to double bluff and treble bluff and so on indefinitely. Is there no change in technique which will rescue the art from becoming stale, and passing out of fashion, like the comedy of manners, through sheer iteration?

One device has been tried lately for altering the formula,

which first took shape in *Murder off Miami*. In that book the reader was presented, as far as possible, with facsimiles of the actual clues which the detective had to work on; type-written documents, spent matches, locks of hair and so on; accurate photographs replaced the familiar sketch-map which used to give you the position of the windows, the fire-place, the roll-top desk and the place where the body was found. The experiment, as an experiment, was quite successful; but somehow I doubt whether its technique could ever become general. The public would begin to demand more and more of it, would want to have the mystery enacted under its very eyes, till at last we should be in the position of that blameless military officer in Chesterton's *Club of Queer Trades*, who looked over a garden fence and saw on the other side of it a bed of tulips so laid out as to read DEATH TO MAJOR BROWN—the work of an agency which undertook to supply romance in real life. We should always be getting mysterious parcels with old boots and things in them, which would turn out to be part of the serial we were following at the moment. Reading, in this fatigued age, is exacting enough without having complications like that.

Some hold that the future of the art lies in a closer approximation to the manner of the ordinary novel. The public no longer expects that a detective story should be badly written; and some of Miss Sayers' work, in particular, is so rich in atmosphere that you could almost forgive her if you found out, as the story proceeded, that she was not bothering to put in a mystery at all. May I register, however, one rather hesitant protest? I do not very much like this modern habit of introducing a *motiv* which found no place in the earlier stories— there is but a single instance of it, I think, in the Holmes cycle —that of illicit love? Not, I hasten to add, from any Victorian prudery on my part, but simply because I believe that in the great battle of wits between the writer and the reader this intrusion of life's backstairs introduces an element of unfair mystification. Where the nub of the problem seems to lie in finding a motive for the crime, it is unsatisfactory to be told, in the last chapter, that this motive lay in a liaison between two characters, a liaison whose existence the reader has had no opportunity of suspecting. But, even apart from this consideration, I do not myself believe that detective fiction has much to learn from the technique of the ordinary novel. Heaven help us, when the psychological crowd are let loose on it.

I hope, nevertheless, that the detective novel will last out my time; so pleasant to read, and not altogether unpleasant to write. When I have no longer any use for relaxation or for royalties, my present audience or any other set of justifiably irritated people is welcome to abolish it. There will be other art-forms, and I suppose they will do just as well.

BELLOC'S VERSE

WILL the fame of Belloc represent him as a writer of verse, or as a writer of prose?

Long ago, at school, I competed for a poetry prize in which Arthur Benson was the examiner. He said to me, "Go on writing poems; you will find it helps you to write prose." The advice came from a suspect source; many people would have said that Arthur Benson had missed his vocation. But what do they think of themselves, these people who write poetry with one hand, and prose with the other? And what ought we to think of them? The list, in our literature, is a surprisingly long one; you can name (at various levels of achievement), Donne, Milton, Dryden, Addison, Southey, Coleridge, Macaulay, Landor, Newman, Matthew Arnold, Stevenson, Walter de la Mare, Mr. Siegfried Sassoon; nor, evidently, is such a list complete. Does a man who possesses this gift of ambidexterity think of himself as a poet who occasionally condescends to prose? Or as a prose-writer who sometimes dabbles in verse? And which medium, in either case, best betrays the true man?

The subject of fame bothered Belloc; he has written of it, and in those later days when his mind was apt to chew the cud of earlier meditations, it recurred in his talk continually. What was this curious illusion which the human mind can neither analyse, nor renounce? I think if he had been offered the choice whether he would rather be remembered by his prose or by his verse, he would have chosen the latter. He used to say that of all his books only four really satisfied him— I am not sure which, but *Belinda* would certainly have been named among them. It was his affectation to talk, sometimes, as if he wrote only for money; poverty and the publishers never allowed him to "linger in his rightful garden"—that of verse.

Verse he called it, not out of modesty, I think, but because he was old-fashioned enough to think of poetry as something which must be polished and repolished until it was perfect in form. This does him no good with the moderns; our critics, in every kind of art, will only let us admire what is flung at us as a smudge, supposedly representing some impression in the artist's mind, all the better for being shapeless. To smell of the midnight oil damns you. Of such contemporary movements Belloc shewed little consciousness, although *The Missing Masterpiece* gives us a hint of what he thought about them. His, in any case, was the classical tradition, deeply rooted in him as in Maurice Baring, though in either case it was difficult to see whence it had sprung. He always talked as if they had taught him precious little Latin and Greek at the Oratory, but his letters written at the time make us hesitate to accept his estimate. I have a copy of *Caliban* in which he inscribed two very mournful lines from the Iliad, with four wrong (but quite plausible) accents to shew that he did not copy the quotation out of a book. He belonged to that period, that culture, in which a receptive mind refreshed itself, almost unconsciously, at the spring of the Classics.

The same influence penetrated into his style, derivatively, through his admiration of French poetry, and especially that of the Augustan period. When he wanted an instance of superlatively good literature, he referred you to *Le Misanthrope*. Of our own poets I think his favourite, in spite of a profound divergence of temperament, was Milton.

In architecture he proclaimed, tirelessly, the Gothic, in literature, it seems to me, all his feeling was for the baroque, its marble simplicity, its dignified restraint. If you want to place him among English poets, you must not put him side

by side with his contemporaries, or even with the Victorians.
He belongs to the classical period which began with Milton,
and ended (for most of us) with Gray.

He belongs to the classical period in his mastery of cadence.
By which I mean, not a mere manipulation of sounds, with a
musical effect, quite divorced from the sense of what you are
saying, and sometimes compelling you to say it unconvincingly
—you get it *ad nauseam* in Swinburne. I mean that perfect
marriage of sound and sense which now and again, especially
in the rounding-off of a poem, creates a kind of stillness in the
mind. Such lines, I mean as:

> They also serve, who only stand and wait,

or:

> And universal darkness buries all.

It is not unknown, to be sure, in recent poetry—Housman
knew the magic of it—but Belloc is continually achieving it.
In such lines, I mean, as:

> . . . but having seen that stone
> (Which was your image), ride more slowly on,

or:

> And her lips virginal,
> Her virginal white feet,

or (with a devastatingly conversational effect):

> On with my coat and out into the night.

There may be those who are unmoved by such effects; who
think them artificial, thought up. Certainly the moderns have
no use for them. I only note that they were dear to the
Augustans, and to Belloc.

He belongs to the classical period in the strong intellectual
background of his poetry. I do not mean that he set out to
mystify us, as the metaphysical poets did, or Browning. I mean

that he was nearly always trying to *say* something; he would not be content merely to record an impression. And this again distinguishes him from the moderns, though not so certainly from the Victorians. But it is more noticeably true of the older poets; there was brain in what they wrote. Consider, for instance, that a competent schoolboy could write you an intelligible *précis* of Gray's *Elegy*; all the magic and the music would be gone, but you would learn what the poem was about. But a schoolboy's *précis* which began "The author declares his intention of going to Innisfree and building nine bean-rows there" would leave no impression on the mind at all. There is brain in the verses Belloc wrote, even (very noticeably) in his nonsense verses, where you might have expected him to leave it behind. He must build; he could not be merely receptive.

He belongs to the classical period because he was, by instinct and by taste, a satirist. It is a curious fact that among the English poets who were his predecessors (unless you regard *Hudibras* as poetry, or Byron as satire) only two were professional satirists, Dryden and Pope. Both used the heroic couplet, with its bite, its detachment, its finality. And in this sort Belloc was—or could have been—a master. This does not appear only in his epigrams, although it is most noticeable in his epigrams. I doubt if the possibilities of the heroic couplet have ever been exploited more fully than in the lines:

> The accurséd power which stands on Privilege
> (And goes with Women, and Champagne, and Bridge)
> Broke—and Democracy resumed her reign:
> (Which goes with Bridge, and Women, and Champagne).

But he used it at length in "To Dives", and returned to it for his "Heroic Poem in Praise of Wine". You may call it *pastiche*, if you will, when he writes a perfect couplet like:

> The dank despisers of the Vine arise
> To watch grey dawns, and mourn indifferent skies

but to be capable of such *pastiche* is to be capable of something beyond mere imitation. One who could so master the secret of Dryden and Pope could, given the opportunity, have written as they did.

"Given the opportunity"—the phrase recalls us to our original question, "Will Belloc be remembered as poet, or as a prose-writer?" Probably as a prose-writer, for no better reason than that his verse output was, by comparison, so small. Ordinarily, the reading public demands a certain level of industry before it will admit a poet to the privileges of immortality; Gray is the shining exception who proves the rule. It is with Belloc as with Johnson; his prose so notably exceeds his verse in mere volume that he is likely to be remembered as a prose-writer who occasionally tried his hand at verse. In his own estimation he was a poet *manqué*; Mr. Sheed, who questioned him directly on the subject, ascertained that this was the meaning of his phrase,

> Nor even in my rightful garden lingered;

and the context of the line (it occurs at the end of "Stanzas Written on Battersea Bridge") shews that he felt it as a grievance. England (and perhaps at the back of his mind he meant Oxford) had refused him something; the leisure to write what he would, as he would. If (*per impossibile*) he had been content to get a Civil Service job on going down from Balliol, he might have dedicated to the Muses those long evenings during which the Inland Revenue had no use for him. As it was, his time and talents were (he felt) being prostituted to the claims of editor and publisher who wanted copy and were content with his second best.

He was, as I have indicated, a man who could not be satisfied with the verse he had written until it had been polished and repolished, recast perhaps, in its perfect form. In his early days, he was no doubt resigned to the experience of not getting things finished, and put it down to his own indolence. You get the echo of such feelings at the beginning of the *Path to Rome*: "What about that little lyric on Winchelsea that you thought of writing six years ago? Why are the lines still in your head and not on paper? Because you can't begin. However, never mind, you can't help it; it's your one great flaw, and it's fatal." When, in middle life, he found that he was still lecturing, still working at biographies which did not really interest him, he felt a grievance about not being allowed to get on with his poetry. The "Heroic Poem in Praise of Wine" was finished late and with difficulty; the "Ode to the West Wind", of which some fragments were already in his mind, never got finished at all. He had produced a respectable number of sonnets, but he was not sure of them; the number of them varies from edition to edition, as if his own judgement had become more exacting. For the rest there was more variety than bulk in his output, unless you included the nonsense verse. If staying-power enters into the definition of a poet, if he must needs put up a brass plate that says "poet" at his front door, Belloc is not among the poets. It is even doubtful whether, on those terms, he would have wished to be. It is impossible to doubt that the different characters in *The Four Men* are in a sense Belloc's own selves, and for the Poet he has an evident though a kindly contempt.

There is another consideration which may, I think, prejudice Belloc's chances of being ranked among the immortals. Rightly or wrongly, we think of each poet as having a vein or genius of his own; his moods may alter, his mannerisms may grow upon him, but there is something in his outlook upon life which remains constant and recognizable. Quite apart from any question of metre or diction, we should give no marks at all to a schoolboy who guessed that "The Scholar Gipsy" was by Swinburne, or "Abt Vogler" by Housman. Belloc, when he sat down to write poetry, had a genius, a vein of his own, like the rest of them. (Chesterton had a feeling for Battersea, but he would not have written the Stanzas on Battersea Bridge.) But a great deal of what Belloc wrote in verse was written without sitting down; scribbled on the back of an envelope or extemporized when there were songs being sung. And so inspired was he, even in his most irresponsible moments, that you cannot write off these lesser effusions of his, like the Juvenilia of Tennyson, or the tameness of Keats in his lighter moods. He will always be judged, to a great extent, by fugitive pieces which, in a collected edition of his own works, he would have polished or suppressed.

The truth is he was too many-sided a man to put only a part of himself into anything he wrote. His gift was for satire; but it is the business of your satirist to be quite inhuman, never to drop the mask of scorn which divides him from his readers. Belloc would drop the mask without warning. The last few pages of *Emmanuel Burden* are as good as anything in English prose, but they are innocent of satire. So with the "Ballade of Illegal Ornaments", which begins as a light-hearted commentary on the ecclesiastical happenings of the day, and ends up, as we know:

> Prince Jesus, in mine Agony,
>   Permit me, broken and defiled,
> Through blurred and glazing eyes to see
>   A Female Figure with a Child.

The *volte-face* is enormously effective, but it disconcerts the conscientious editor who is determined to label the poems and divide them up into sections according to the mood in which they were written. Sometimes, of course, the *volte-face* will be the other way round:

Prince, on their iron thrones they sit,
~~Impassible to our despair,~~
The dreadful Guardians of the Pit;—
And Mrs. Roebeck will be there.

What is the fellow about? Is he to be taken seriously, or with a grain of salt? Is he to be classed with Rabelais, or with George Herbert? Criticism does not love the unpredictable.

Actually, it may be doubted whether Belloc was not too much of a humorist to be a straight satirist, and *vice versa*. The satirist, for the sake of contrast, ought to take himself seriously; in Belloc, there was a streak of humility which let down the average—he could laugh at himself. I still picture him, one New Year's eve, reading aloud to his family my brother's parody of his own poem on Sussex, and shouting with laughter. You are not prepared for his sudden condescensions to the ludicrous—as when you find, among his published sonnets, one which begins,

Would that I had £300,000.

Contrariwise, as I have suggested above, the trouble about his nonsense verses is that they are so full of good sense. When Lear writes nonsense, or Lewis Carroll, you find only a jingle of sounds, which has nothing in common with serious poetry except rhyme and metre. When Belloc sat down to the same task, the imp of satire was for ever perched on his shoulder; and there is a whole world of social history in such lines as:

The people in between
Looked underdone and harassed,
And commonplace and mean,
And horribly embarrassed.

I read *The Modern Traveller* as a boy, and loved it; so too, as a boy, I read *Gulliver's Travels*, and loved them; but in the one case as the other, I was never really conscious of what it was all about. You cannot divide up Belloc's poetry, as you can divide up Hood's, into Serious and Comic; the two qualifications overlap and interlock; in letters, as in life, the severity of his lips is pulled downwards, all of a sudden, into a smile.

To make him all the more unclassifiable, Belloc was a songwriter. This is a trick quite distinct from poetry; the Elizabethans had it, but it is rare among the moderns. Belloc was one of those people who, perhaps to work off their high spirits, perhaps to conceal their low spirits, will for ever be bursting into song. I remember his driving me from Arundel to King's Land, singing at the wheel all the way. And when his repertoire failed, he would make up songs of his own, sometimes with tunes of his own, a feat hardly imaginable in Pope, say, or Wordsworth. If every other record of him should perish, it is to be hoped that posterity will be able to hear, on a gramophone record, "Ha'nacker Mill" as it was sung by its own author and composer. That last haunting line, "Never a ploughman. Never a one" will perpetuate his genius, and his sadness. But how to place him? How to rank "Ha'nacker Mill" among the other classics?

Nullum fere scribendi genus non tetigit, nullum quod tetigit non ornavit; is it only Goldsmith that deserves the epitaph? And is there no immortality for the versatile?

BIRMINGHAM REVISITED

IT IS alleged by a friend of my family that I used to suffer from insomnia at the age of four; and that when she asked me how I managed to occupy my time at night I answered "I lie awake and think of the past." This early habit of reminiscence must, I suppose, be the title which has singled me out as a contributor to this series of revisitations. For indeed, I can only boast myself a Birmingham man by adoption, and even so by fits and starts. I am a son of the manse, and clerical families are always on the move; further, if you go to school at a distance, and spend your summer holiday in the country, you do not see a great deal of your native, or putatively native town. Yet Birmingham was all that the word "home" meant to me from the age of four to the age of fifteen, the time of life at which that word means most; and as I approach Snow Hill by the railway the dingy brick arcading that faces the embankment still evokes, by the very sight of it, an illusory lightness of the heart; it means coming home for the holidays.

When I left Birmingham in 1903 I left it for Manchester, and hastened to transform myself from a Birmingham boy into a Lancashire lad. There is thus a kind of impudent appropriateness in the fact that I am broadcasting at this moment from the Manchester station. The habits of the carpet-bagger still cling to me, pardonable in a politician, and even honourable in a professional footballer, but a poor qualification for the revisitor. I can only plead that Birmingham does not actually produce the men whom she delights to honour. The Cadburys, to be sure, are indigenous; but James Watt came from Greenock, Joseph Priestley from the West Riding, John

Bright from Rochdale, and Joseph Chamberlain, if the horrid truth must be told, was a Londoner born and bred. True to her manufacturing instincts, Birmingham is not concerned with the raw product of notability; she takes over the unfinished article, moulds it, refines it, and re-exports it dignified, for ever, with her trade-mark.

Four out of those eleven years of my boyhood were spent not in Birmingham itself but at Aston, of which parish my father was vicar. When I revisited Birmingham the other day, I attempted to walk to Aston, and found the distance, unlike most of the distances we remember from childhood, too much for me. (I associate that journey with a family habit, hygienic doubtless but uncomfortable, of walking over in later years all the way from St. Philip's Rectory to Aston Church, to attend the afternoon service on Christmas Day. I associate it, more gratefully, with the old steam-trams with their broad cow-catchers, the engine a separate vehicle linked by a chain to the tram proper, which covered that distance at such a majestic pace in the nineties.) This time, I only got as far as the clock-tower that stands in the middle of the road, painted green now, though I think it was red in the nineties, the South Pole, in those early days, of all pedestrian expeditions. Aston, I hope, remains just as it was; the Vicarage garden with the big copper-beech tree and the brewery chimney overlooking it; Aston Park, with the trees, aged since then but surely not fallen, between which I played Tom Tiddler's Ground, and Aston Hall with the cannon-balls Cromwell shot at it, and the stuffed lion in the entrance, regarding new generations of children with the same glassy eye. If these things have changed, I would rather not hear about it. The people will have changed, but I don't remember them much. One went out to Gravelly Hill, to call on a Miss Morrison and a Miss Henn; one of them, I think it was Miss Henn, still played on the harp as a drawing-room accomplishment. On the other hand, I remember a

Colonel Brody—was it Brody? some name like that—who kept a phonograph; an instrument which recorded the human voice on cylindrical rolls, and must have been the parent, I suppose, of the gramophone. Thus my musical memories of the period divide themselves into gracious contact with the past, and a horrible presage of the future.

But nobody wants this personal stuff; what was I saying? Oh yes, that I hope Aston hasn't changed. Certainly the road to Aston hasn't; except for one church and one cinema, there was no building between that clock-tower and Gosta Green which had not passed under the scrutiny of a small face pressed against the window of the steam-tram; the same endearing ugliness of Victorian brick façades; the same queer alternations in the level of the pavement. I confess that my chief impression of Birmingham itself, that is of Birmingham proper, is a surprising absence of change. In Broad Street there is a War Memorial, with a sort of abbreviated park round it, which naturally is since my time; the hospital has been enlarged, but it is the same hospital; and when I went down the arcade I found the same toy-shop which I used to haunt, with the same name over the door—I wanted to pat a small would-be purchaser on the shoulder, and assure him "Et ego in Arcadia vixi." Snow Hill was already being altered, I think, when we left; and as for New Street, I like to think it hasn't had so much as a lick of paint in this century.

That is the odd thing about the great Victorian cities. The central part of them was put up in times when man built badly but solidly, and had no idea of town-planning. And the sites are just not valuable enough to make it worth while pulling down those awful structures; so they remain, with all their familiar grotesqueness, for the revisitor to gloat over. A place like Oxford looks changed at the beginning of every year; Birmingham remains. To be sure, if you approach it by road, as I have approached it, from Knowle on the south or Oscott

on the north, you pass through miles and miles of that bunga-
low civilization which seems to argue that men have forgotten
how to share doorsteps, or climb up a flight of stairs. But all
this is only accretion; the city itself remains, a fly in amber.

I cannot profess that my memories even of that restricted
area, Birmingham proper, are photographically accurate. I have
a bad sense of topography, and am probably the only person
who even in youth, even on a dark night, has lost his way
between St. Philip's Church and St. Philip's Rectory. That
church and that rectory are the centre of all my associations;
my father became rector there in 1895. The rectory stands
at the further end of the churchyard; sandwiched, in those
days, between the Bank of England and the Bluecoat school,
Mammon on one side and charity on the other, with an air of
not letting its left hand know what its right hand did. I am
sorry to find that the Bluecoat school has been pulled down,
and that the window of my old bedroom is thus exposed to
the profane eyes of Colmore Row, until they put up the
monstrous hotel or whatever it is they are going to build there.
I say I am sorry the school has been pulled down; for I remember it as a pleasant place in the eighteenth-century manner,
with tailor's models of the inmates standing by the front door.
But I am not really sorry that those boys are kicking their
heels in the suburbs, instead of walking across solemnly, as
they used to, to their pews in the gallery of St. Philip's every
Sunday morning. The yard where I and my three brothers
played was none too large for us; and our footballs were
constantly having to be retrieved from the back premises of
the Great Western Arcade at the back. The school playground
was naturally larger, but it must have been a tight fit for the
mob of boys whose shouts came to us over the side wall.

As for the church, it is outside what it always was; inside,
they have taken out the pews and put in chairs and an extra
Communion-table without, to my mind, creating in the least

degree the illusion of a cathedral. It was more of a piece as
it was; those pews in which kneeling was hardly possible;
those raised pews, best of all, at the back, for the rector and
the wardens, where you were concealed from the public gaze
when you were hunting for the threepence that had escaped
through the glove that had a hole in it, but could peep over,
comfortably, at the thrilling moment when the frock-coated
sidesmen, reunited at last, began their solemn march, full-
handed, up the nave. I suppose Burne-Jones' stained-glass
windows are not really stained-glass windows, but what colour!
And in those days, colour was the only thing that really
mattered.

On your right, as you looked from the Rectory windows,
was Colmore Row. I believe I can remember the crowds there,
and the shouting, on the night when an eminent statesman, still
alive to-day and still volcanically active, escaped from his
Imperialist critics only, it was said, by disguising himself as a
policeman. Where it joined St. Philip's Place, the cable trams
started; not so monumental, not so friendly as the steam trams
of Aston days, but fascinating from the mystery of their progress. You could stand, until you were torn away by anxious
relatives, half-way between the lines, and look down through
the slit into which the trams put their feelers, catching sight,
if you were lucky, of the moving rope underneath. Electric
trams had already started, but only in the Bristol Road; there
was fine plunging motion if you sat in front at the top, almost
recalling the perils of the sea.

Beyond Colmore Row was Barwick Street, where I learned
to bicycle; the machine I used, family property, had only one
tyre and that of solid rubber. (I think it was in Broad Street
that I stared, round-eyed, at my first sight of a motor; but the
traffic in Birmingham was already dangerous for an absent-
minded rider like myself.) Or if you went along Colmore
Row you came to the Town Hall and the Art Gallery and the

fountain in the Square with the plaque of Mr. Chamberlain; all that was magnificent, and I am fond of the Town Hall still. Beyond that again was Broad Street, an interminable stretch, it seemed, leading up to Five Ways, where you demanded a Shrewsbury cake as the reward of your exertions, unless you had lightened your labours by climbing onto one of the single-horse 'buses which paraded decorously along it. All beyond that was Edgbaston, where people lived whom you had to visit in clean collars. Of the Oratory I knew nothing; I think I was once taken into St. Chad's, but carried no impression away except that of innumerable candles.

On the right St. Philip's churchyard, if I may take you back to that, was bounded by Temple Row, with its air of being inhabited by respectable lawyers; and from this a network of little roads, Cherry Street and Needless Alley and so on, led down to Corporation Street and New Street; very puzzling I used to find them, though they seem plain enough now. I cannot get over a certain sense of personal injury when I find that Corporation Street has now a one-way system of traffic. It is as if a Londoner should find himself forbidden to go West-wards along the Strand. New Street Station afflicts me, even now, with a sense of vertigo, so often have I lost my bearings among its multitudinous platforms. My favourite memories are of Platform Four, I think it is, where I used to dodge the sham policeman who was supposed to take the bicycle tickets. I collected railway tickets in those days; and when you were returning from a country ride to Lichfield or Kenilworth or Coventry or one of those jolly little country towns, it gave you a fine thrill to ride past at full speed, pretending deafness to his protests.

That was all my Birmingham really, though of course there were the show places—Bingley Hall, where people walked on the tight-rope, and Cannon Hill Park, with the boating and the swans. Oh, and the football; I had nearly forgotten the football. Conscientious patriotism would take us, sometimes, to watch Small Heath (I think they call it "Birmingham" now) or even West Bromwich Albion, where they sold thick ham sandwiches and lemon cheesecakes on the ground. But primarily, of course, we were Villa fans; and I can still see the enormous advertisement of tyres which ran round the enclosure, "First in 1888, foremost ever since"—it was the year of my own birth, so I was apt to draw fallacious omens from it; still feel the panic of the human squeeze when you were swept out through the gates. Devey, and Athersmith, and Cowan, and Crabtree—I suppose those heroes of my youth now go unremembered. But I have stood on the seat, believe it or not, booing the referee when I suspected him of being unduly influenced by the claims of Liverpool; a feeling which seemed generally shared, though indeed claret-and-light-blue had the better of scarlet by five goals to nothing. That seems a long time ago.

Has Birmingham changed? Not much, I think; certainly not in its outward appearance; certainly not in its politics; certainly not in its air of cheerful bustle and tentative refinement. But man is the measure of all things; and in this case I am myself the measure by which Birmingham is judged. Could I really boo a referee nowadays? Could I still feel enthusiastic about the stuffed lion? It is a dreadful confession, but I feel as if it must be I, not Birmingham, that has changed.

FRENCH WITH TEARS

I HAVE no idea why I am being allowed to deliver this lecture. It has no sort of connexion either with the kind of things I ordinarily talk about, or with the kind of things people ordinarily come to listen about. It does not convey any information about the French language, or French literature, or the French people, or their history or their present place in the world order, which anybody did not know before. It propounds no thesis, aims at no conclusion. It is simply an autobiography; that of an ordinary middle-class person who has learned French in the ordinary middle-class way. And to that autobiography is appended the question, to which no answer is given, How is it that a person who has spent such a comparatively large part of his life in learning French, reading French, going to France even on occasion, and listening to people talk French, is a non-starter whenever conversation has to be conducted in that language, either in mixed company or *tête-à-tête* (by which I mean head to head). At the very end I shall suggest the thought that it is a bad thing to have so many Englishmen like me going about, incapable of talking French, in view of the obvious fact that, when you cut the cackle, the peace of the world depends on Englishmen and Frenchmen understanding one another.

I begin, then, with my autobiography as a Gallicist. I never had a French governess; there were never meal-times in my family during which conversation had to be conducted in French, nor did any person of French extraction, that I heard of, darken our doors. When did I start learning French? I cannot even remember. I started Greek when I was seven, before I ever went to school; and the fact that the crocodile moves its upper jaw remains with me to this day. But it sticks in my head that I must have started French also before I went to school; and the reminiscence is associated with the irregular verbs, and particularly the verb *bouillir*, by which I mean the French for "to boil". I must, I think, have resented learning that verb. No doubt it is a useful verb enough; in a hot sun one might want to say, "C'est bouillant, n'est-ce pas?" or, when dressing for dinner, you might have to ask a French servant, "Où est ma chemise bouillie?" I am conjugating the verb by memory, and I daresay wrongly. Anyhow, there were too many vowels about it for me, and that must, I think, have led to tears, and so fixed the beastly word in my memory.

It can hardly be imagined, though, that I fleshed my teeth entirely on paradigms. I suppose it was at this time that I went through the Ollendorffian curriculum which was then usual, and may for all I know be usual to-day. A system which made it possible for you to translate the Degrees of Kindred and Affinity at the end of the prayer-book into French without a murmur—"La belle cousine", etc. A system which provided you with a Gallic rendering for most of the primary necessities of life, from pens, ink, and paper upwards, though commonly attributing the ownership of such articles to the gardener, or at least to his wife. The French, for whom it will be observed as this paper proceeds that I have a profound admiration, have one fault in the Englishman's eyes—they aren't really interested in gardening; seldom keep gardens, except round very big houses, if the evidence of the railway-carriage window is to be trusted. And whereas nobody is more ready than myself, in a general way, to subscribe to the maxim that they order these things better in France, nobody who has received a letter from that country can have failed to observe that their paper is vile, their ink watery, and their pens scratchy, in a degree which would not be tolerated over here. Strange, then, and perhaps characteristic of the insular lines on which our education used to be conducted, that the first words we learned to stammer in French were an appeal to be provided with the three things which France, least of all countries, is able to provide, and those three the property of a functionary whose duties were presumably a sinecure.

And yet perhaps it might be argued that those early sentence books do contrive, with an uncanny knack of characterization, to sum up for you the atmosphere of the civilization you are studying. *Ho krokodeilos ten ano gnathon kinei*, The crocodile moves his upper jaw—typical of that spirit of enquiry with which the Greek genius first taught us to investigate the secrets of nature. *Balbus aedificavit murum*, Balbus built a wall; and in doing so he was a typical Roman; shewed the spirit of the imperial race which ordered our civilization for us, its military instinct, its slow, cautious method of procedure; something too of that love of exact definition which gave us laws. "Donnez-moi la plume, l'encre, et le papier du jardinier"— the Frenchman revealed himself, in that sentence, as the victim of a restless literary ambition which must express itself at all costs; yet would express itself with the neatness, the concinnity, the ordered precision which distinguishes a culti- vated garden from a romantic forest—Corneille from Keats. But I digress.

The excellent preparatory school to which I was sent specialized in getting classical scholarships at Eton; and any- body who shewed promise in Latin and Greek was early seconded for intensive tuition in those subjects. Such was my own fate; yet it does not appear that the French language figured in my own mind as a side-show. I recovered some time back the fragments of a diary kept when I was just turning eleven, little more than a year before I went in for the Eton scholarship; and I not only find under February the 9th the entry "Full marks"—not top marks, notice, full marks—"for French grammar"; but I see that I have written in the words "Mardi Gras" on Feb. 14th, and "Mercredi des cendres" on Feb. 15th. If you had asked me, I should have told you that I took no interest at that age except in Latin verses; but this document belies the data of memory. Fifty-two years ago, I must have thought of myself as a promising French scholar.

The credit for this (alas! transitory) enthusiasm I give wholly to Bam. Bam was our French master; his real name was Mr. Evans, and the origin of his cultus title was lost in antiquity. I can see him yet with singular clearness, as one sees the pictures of those days; a little man in a light-grey suit, with a shining bald head, prominent cheeks, a pointed grey beard, and demi-lunettes (the very thought of him rekindles, you see, my old ardour)—I mean those spectacles which are cut off square at the top so as only to cover the lower half of the eyes, while the upper half peered at you with a permanent twinkle that expressed at once eagerness for his subject, and contempt for his pupils. He would shake his book at us as we gave wrong answers to some question that had us all guessing, while he rapped out, "Jamais—jamais—jamais!" at each in turn. But the most withering expression he used, when he could find no other formula in which to sum up the incompetence of our efforts, was, "Yer might as well come out to play cricket with a golf-stick." No athlete myself, I felt cut to the quick whenever this curious analogy was employed.

What Bam's origins were, I have no idea; he certainly spoke English oddly, and was perhaps just a Welshman. We all believed that he was of mixed Belgian and Irish blood; and there were those who maintained that he was in reality a Papist, only going to chapel (where he never sang in the choir) for fear of losing his job. But there was a foreign flourish about him; his pointed beard and (if the truth must be told) his liberal use of a tooth-pick after meals surrounded him with an

aura of the Quartier Latin. You will observe that the subject
in which I got full marks was French *grammar*; and it is certain
that we memorized painfully, not only *genou hibou joujou pou*
and *chacal pal regal*, but an interminable list of masculines
ending in E mute. *Bouillir* had no further terrors for me; I
could have met a Frenchman and said to him "that thou
mightest boil thyself" without turning a hair. But it was not
only the dry bones we assimilated; if I re-read the *Bourgeois
Gentilhomme* to-day, I should hear in all its choicest phrases the
mocking accents of little Bam. When I was about to leave, he
told me that I knew French as well as anybody could possibly
know it at my age without having been to France. If you make
the important addition "and without having ever heard French
talked, except in class", I am inclined to think he was right.

Unfortunately in those days I was a convinced pot-hunter;
and when I went to Eton and found people there who had been
to France or talked French to governesses, I saw that prizes in
this field were beyond my reach, and slacked off accordingly.
I now came under the tuition of a Frenchman, M. Cuvelier,
who was regrettably nick-named "Cow-belly". A sad man
with a drooping sandy moustache; very kind-hearted, but
incapable of arousing enthusiasm. We believed that he had
been an exile ever since the Franco-Prussian war, when he had
escaped from a fortress and swum the Rhine under a hail of
enemy bullets; but the historicity of the setting seems doubtful, and if he had seen military service in 1870, he must have
been well preserved. The important fact about him here can
be expressed in three words; he was ragged. If I could recall
details about the savagery with which he was treated, I would
not have the heart to produce them in this lecture. I have too
clear a vision of what a ragged schoolmaster's life must be, to
make humorous capital out of its tragedy. I learnt nothing, I
am afraid, in those French classes (chiefly devoted to the
intolerable Marbot), except a number of disconnected pieces

of general knowledge, from a book of French compositions, by one Barrère. Curious, how many of the facts one knows are really derived from old French exercises. Cow-belly was the only master who was supposed to take me in French until, in the upper part of the school, I came under the influence of M. Hua. This was a little man with a heavy black beard and a comedian's manner, and there was a legend about him which endeared him to the imagination. Late at night, it was said, M. Hua let himself out of his lodgings in the High Street, and knocked at a little secret door in the wall of Windsor Castle; and there, discreetly admitted, he sat till the small hours of the morning telling dirty stories to King Edward VII. He was not ragged, but he was a lax disciplinarian; and I cannot remember learning anything from him except, once more by way of composition pieces, the history of the top hat (which he made us translate "huit-reflets", that is, "eight reflections"). It was invented by a hatter called Etherington, pronounced Etherington by M. Hua. It was originally of a round, bell-like shape; and when Etherington went out into the street wearing it rude boys shouted after him "Who's your hatter?" Thus does Eton prepare us for the great battle of life.

There was also a system known as classical French, which meant that you construed a French book to your ordinary form master, I think twice a week. Such a lesson is admirably described in the first chapter of Mr. Maurice Baring's novel, *Friday's Business*. This only taught you to read French; not to write, still less to speak it. I can remember revelling in Monte Cristo, and, more surprisingly, in Daudet's *Contes de Lundi*. I once selected as a prize, at the age of fourteen, the plays of Corneille, of which I read three or four painstakingly, as you do at that age; the only line I remember is "Et de ses propres mains déchire ses entrailles". I read also before I left school one or two other plays by Victor Hugo and Rostand; but I never really loved French poetry, because it always seemed to me to cheat over the E mute; lines wouldn't scan until you had counted the syllables. If I were fond of giving advice to the young (which I am not, because they never take it), I would say, Read all you can for pleasure before you are twenty-five; after that, you will only read for profit or for relaxation. Since I left school, I have never read French for the sake of reading French.

But naturally I have read a good deal of French one way and another. Nor am I ashamed to admit that I find French infinitely the best language, I had almost said the only possible language, for spiritual reading. I have got through seven or eight of the late Abbé Bremond's admirable volumes, each of them six hundred pages or so, bearing a title which may be roughly translated "A Literary History of the Religious Sentiment in France". I do not think anybody except a Frenchman could make a long chronicle of the various mystics or semi-mystics his country had produced into a book as readable as a novel. Not that I do read French novels. For one thing, the words in them are too hard; and for another thing . . . well, French has such a curious way of making things look indelicate even when they're really quite all right. I had a detective story of mine translated into French not long ago; it was published by a Belgian firm which caters for a specially Catholic public, and it was seen through the press by a Jesuit. Well, one of the chapters in my story was called, "An Eloping Race"; rather a good idea, really, but I can't stop to explain it. And when I opened one of my presentation copies, with the legitimate pride you feel when you achieve publicity of this sort, what should my eye light on but a chapter heading which read, "La Chasse au Ravisseur". Well, really I mean, was that the only way of translating it?

I am not a reader of French novels, but I claim that I can read French. Moreover, I can understand French when it is spoken, within limits. I don't make the effort to follow a

French conversation between two other people. But I can make pretty good time with a lecture or a sermon, or even with conversation addressed to me, as long as it doesn't exceed the speed limit. I have even heard confessions in French, without having to fall back on the ingenious expedient of that legendary English priest who, after listening to a stream of voluble self-accusation without understanding one word of it, drew himself up judicially and said, "Oh, vous avez, avez-vous?" This being so, or seeming to me to be so, my point is, Why is it that I can't speak French?

Why is it that when I leave the train at Paris I find myself, like most of my fellow-countrymen, unable to get further than the useful phrase, "Ou est le Cook's homme?" Why is it that, whereas I could make some shift to talk Greek to Plato or Latin to Cicero in the unlikely event of my meeting either of them, I found myself completely tongue-tied when I was introduced to M. Maritain? I sat through a whole luncheon party at Balliol some years ago, in which the conversation was conducted entirely in French; and not a word could I get out till the scout—he had been my own scout years ago, and was as familiar to me as the Martyrs' Memorial—tried to make me eat some fruit salad, and I said "Merci" by mistake.

Of course, it may be only an individual kink of mine; or it may be the fault of my age, for after all I was brought up in the bad old days before the Great War. Perhaps the ordinary Englishman of to-day can prattle in French without effort. But my impression is that I speak for many others besides myself when I ask, What is this strange inhibition that makes us unable to talk to a Frenchman? Note you, we are expected to talk French when we go to France, even on a short visit. The French themselves, if they are paying a short visit to England, never dream of learning *our* language; have we not spent years informing ourselves, with a precision but incredible, but admirable, how to form the plural of an owl or a louse? Why then, we will be able to speak French to them; what need to indoctrinate oneself with this tongue so barbaric? Thus the French argue; and when they meet me they set me down for a blockhead or a surly brute you cannot get a word out of. Or they talk about this droll English reserve—reserved! me!

Of course, in the first analysis the thing is simple enough. I cannot talk French because I am hopelessly self-conscious. I am afraid of talking it badly. That kind of self-consciousness comes from our public schools. Chesterton has laid it down somewhere that if a thing is worth doing at all it is worth doing badly. And there is a great deal to be said for talking a language badly. In England, certainly, we find the linguistic difficulties of the foreigner—I don't mean, of course, people who have learned to talk English really well—positively attractive. In Oxford, a man who talks English imperfectly can dine out on it for three years. I remember a great friend of my own, now quite an important person in Belgium, who was a case in point. He had the art of talking English badly in its perfection. I remember that when I became a Catholic I met him in London, and broke the news to him with considerable pleasure, as he was one of the very few Catholic friends I then had. His reply was a perfect specimen of half-bad English; "That," he said, "will excite furiously my mother." But your Englishman, and above all your public-school Englishman, hates talking a foreign language, just as he hates making a public speech, for fear he should do it badly. The result is that he always *does* it badly; for the first requisite in talking a foreign language, as in making a public speech, is some measure of self-confidence.

And here, strangely enough, I think you may say that all the French we learned so tearfully at school is not a help, but a positive hindrance. We do not remember how to do it right, but we remember with painful clearness how many ways there are of doing it wrong. There is a famous story that a recent head-master of Rugby, going round the form-rooms on a tour of inspection, went into a French class and was asked, by the discreet master in charge, to "take over", as the military say. And he proceeded to introduce the class to this very profound consideration: "Remember, boys, there are five perfectly distinct sounds in French, On, on, on, on and on." That sort of thing is a great handicap to a man in later life; when he finds himself talking to a Frenchman and embarking, say, on the word "Angleterre" without being quite certain whether the first syllable of it should be on, on, on, on or on. Again, a friend once told me that the French word for "Yes", a word which one is always wanting to use in answer to such questions as "Encore du vin?" is not pronounced WEE as in Wee Macgregor, you ought to make a noise which would be better represented in English by the letters WIH, "Wih!"—like that. As Mark Twain said, foreigners always spell better than they pronounce. And then another friend told me that a Frenchman does not really say Wee, or rather Wih, by itself, but always tacks it onto the end of some other word, "Mais wih" for preference. It is very hard to remember to put that in. I know what you are going to say, yes, it's a perfectly good way out to confine yourself to the use of the word *parfaitement*. But the word *parfaitement* is one which I only remember when I am half-way down the stairs, after taking my *congé* or leave, and it would look silly to go back on purpose to say it.

There is another inhibition which holds me tongue-tied, though perhaps this is an individual consideration which would not apply equally to others. I cannot bear discussing the obvious topic, or saying the obvious things about it; I would always rather remain silent. And the phrases which spring to my mind ready-made, if I am forced into conversation with foreigners, are always the obvious phrases about the obvious things, so that I despise myself for using them. I may be wrong, but I feel as if I could put any amount of that stuff across without serious difficulty. "Il fait joli temps, n'est-ce pas? Je crois qu'en France vous avez le joli temps toujours, mais toujours. En Angleterre il pleut beaucoup; on ne veut jamais sortir sans porter une parapluie, vous savez", and so on and so on, with *n'est-ce pas* and *vous savez* coming in handy whenever you are at a loss for a word. And the worst of it is I believe that I could get away with it, and find myself welcomed as a stimulating companion all over the continent of Europe, if I could bring myself to prattle gaily about that sort of thing. "Quel joli jardin! Je crois que vous avez un très bon jardinier. Moi, j'aime beaucoup les roses; elles sont très jolies, n'est-ce pas? Il y a beaucoup de beaux fleurs dans le jardin de ma tante"—that sort of thing is as easy as falling off a log. But for some mysterious reason I cannot bring myself to do it.

If I were going out for a country walk with a Frenchman, I should find myself immediately wanting to express more sudden and arresting thoughts. I should want to say, for example, "That cow looks rather like a parson I know"—I am merely suggesting that by way of illustration. Well, it ought to be a simple sentence enough. But I am handicapped from the start by the consciousness that it is not what my French friend is expecting me to say; it will have to be done neatly and snappily if I am to get it across. "Cette vache-là", that part is all right; no difficulty about the gender of the beast; fortunately we are not talking German, in which a cow might quite possibly be neuter. "Cette vache-là"—or perhaps better "cette vache-ci" when you come to think of it, this one here, to distinguish it from the other cows which are *là*. "Looks like"—that is much more difficult. The word I want is *ressembler* or *rassembler*, I am not quite sure which; and the other verb, whichever is the wrong one, probably means to reassemble. Also, I cannot for the life of me remember whether it is an ordinary verb or a reflexive verb. It would be

silly to find yourself saying, "That cow reassembles itself."
Happy thought, you can say in French that a thing has the air
of something else. "Cette vache-ci a l'air de"—how does one
put "parson", though? *Prêtre* or *curé* would be misleading;
he would think I meant a Frenchman; *ministre*? But that might
mean a Cabinet minister. "A l'air d'un ministre de religion
de l'église d'Angleterre"; there seem to be too many *de*'s
about this sentence, but it will have to pass. Then "whom I
know"; that is important, or I might be suspected of generaliz-
ing. Now, is it "que je connais" or "qui je connais"?
Panic-stricken, I return to Ollendorff; the gardener whom my
aunt has married, would that be *qui* or *que ma tante a épousé*?
Que, I think; we shall have to risk it anyhow. There, there is
the whole sentence ready to be released: "Cette vache-ci a
l'air d'un ministre de religion de l'église d'Angleterre que je
connais." But by this time *cette vache-ci* is no longer even
cette vache-là; it has disappeared over the horizon. I plod on
in silence. What reserve these English have (my French friend
thinks); how inscrutable is their manner, how profound must
be their meditations!

He never suspects my inability to talk French to him,
because he finds that I can understand him quite tolerably when
he talks French to me. Especially when he talks to me, as
Frenchmen are apt to talk, in wide generalities, such as
demand the use of words derived straight from the Latin.
With a German, I have no difficulty at all. I cannot understand
him, and therefore he does not expect me to talk to him. If
we meet with a cow on our walk, a sudden idea occurs to
me; I point at it, so that there can be no mistake, and say
"Kuh!" I am not sure that it ought not to have a couple of
dots on its back, but it works all right; he bursts into a roar
of laughter; for to the German mind the mere fact of identification has a rich humour-value. Then he makes a great effort,
and says something a bit like "Cow". I take both his hands

in mine, and we stand there, the tears starting to our eyes at this evocation of our Indo-European origins. We are brothers—because I never learnt any German, or he any English, at school.

Whereas I can understand the Frenchman, as I say, quite tolerably. He is, perhaps, an enthusiast who has just started a paper or organized a movement designed to rally the *jeunesse catholique*. He will receive a warm welcome from *M. l'aumôn-ier*, that sees itself easily. He tells me he is sure that the Catholic students of Oxford would wish well to enter into relations more narrow and more fruitful with the universitary Catholics of France, is it not so? And he finds himself of a conviction that the receipt of more frequent and more detailed renseignements about the actual situation in his country, together with the contemporary movements of Catholic thought and a more precise explication of their cultural significance, would operate powerfully to intensify the inter-national accord in which we happily find ourselves since a long time ago. Would I then be willing, in view of my distinguished position as one of the cultural leaders in the great movement of youth towards religion among the universities of England, to become a propagandist for his newspaper, and to facilitate its diffusion among the students of Oxford; perhaps also to enrol them, is it not so, as members either honorary or tributary of his association, which has already made among the students of the French universities a reverberation so profound?

All that I understand, more or less; and the obvious answer is *Non*—or possibly *non, non, non,* or *non*. But it seems dis-courteous, somehow, to meet all that torrent of eloquence with a monosyllable of refusal. If an Englishman, or more probably an American, tried to get at me with that sort of stuff, I would disillusion him gently but firmly; pointing out that Oxford undergraduates are not students in any recogniz-able sense of the word, that they hate reading parish maga-zines, that they loathe belonging to any kind of organization, and even if they do, persistently forget to pay their subscriptions. But I cannot start out, heaven help me, to explain all that in French. So I find myself saying "Wih", or perhaps "Mais wih" if I am in very good form. My intense desire never to meet the man again prevents me climbing up half a flight of stairs to supplement my answer with the word *parfaitement.*

I sometimes wonder whether this sort of thing happens in the higher spheres of international diplomacy. I mean, one is always reading in the newspapers that conversations are being held between the representatives of two European countries; is a conversation held between a French politician and (say) Sir John Simon conducted on the lines I have indicated just now? Does the Frenchman talk at great length about pacts and guarantees and sanctions and reparations and the stabilization of currency and the regulation of imports and international credits and all the rest of it, and does Sir John Simon find himself answering "Wih" in rather the same spirit as myself? And then, lest he might be suspected of a too limited vocabulary, does he follow it up with "Donnez-moi s'il vous plaît une plume, de l'encre, et du papier", and sign the pact or whatever it is without further ado? Is that what is meant when we hear that an understanding has been reached? Probably not; probably Sir John Simon knows quite a lot about foreign languages really. But I do suggest that when the average Englishman meets the average Frenchman the conversation nearly always has to take place in French; that the volubility of the Frenchman reduces the Englishman to an attitude of vague but pleased assent; that the Frenchman, in consequence, always imagines his English friends see eye to eye with him over political and economic questions, and very naturally talks about perfidious Albion when he finds that this impression was mistaken.

I suppose I was brought up in a world in which the French

and English peoples, if not enemies, were the next best thing
to it. When the Fashoda incident occurred I was just ten
years old; about the age at which one begins to realize that
Frenchmen are real, not just people in a book, like the Latins
and Greeks. If the truth must be told, I suppose the ordinary
Englishman felt about France something rather like what he
now feels about Italy; only we had not yet learned to take the
Continent very seriously. A Frenchman was absurd, pompous,
theatrical, and at the same time mischievous and treacherous;
also a coward. I suppose that didn't do much harm, as long
as our foreign policy involved no alliance with France. It is
not very important to understand your enemies; when Pistol
said of his French prisoner, "I will fer him, and firk him, and
ferret him, discourse the same in French unto him", and the
Boy replied, "I do not know the French for fer, and firk, and
ferret", it is probable that the unfortunate foreigner was
nevertheless able to get a line on the attitude of his captor from
his general demeanour. But it is, surely, important to understand one's friends; and indeed I understand that official
efforts are always being made in peace-time to develop more
intimate cultural relations with the continent of Europe
generally. My problem is, how this is to be done where
France is concerned, so long as there hangs over the British
Channel a sea-fog of half-comprehended idiom, such as I have
been trying to depict?

Some years ago now there was an interesting article in that
little-read organ, the *Oxford Magazine*, which set itself to
answer the question, Why do Oxford undergraduates like
Germans better than Frenchmen? The chief cause was, as well
as I remember, that Oxford undergraduates spent their holidays
in Germany to learn the language, because they knew they
didn't know it; but not in France, because they thought that
they knew the language already. That was soon after the Nazis
came into power; I doubt if nowadays the symptoms are so

marked. It remains true, nevertheless, that the average more or less educated Englishman knows he doesn't know German, but thinks he knows French. And as long as that remains true, we are doubly at cross-purposes. The Englishman sits patient under the Frenchman's long tirades, hypnotized by the flood of rhetoric, the gesticulations, the confidential manner, and hoping that he is "more or less getting the hang of it". But as a matter of fact, he is left with a singularly vague impression; is it merely because I am so bad at French, or do others share my feeling that an argument set out in French always seems convincing at the time, and afterwards you find great difficulty in remembering what it was? Meanwhile, the Frenchman is amazed, and secretly appalled, by the Englishman's silence; but my God, how inscrutable, how impenetrable, he says to himself, while the Englishman is simply trying to think up his genders for the next sentence he will get in edgeways. So they part, to all appearance, two minds with but a single thought, but in fact the curse of Babel broods over their leave-taking.

What is to be done about it? I have no remedies to offer. One way, of course, would be for the French, I mean the mass of Frenchmen, to learn some English. Why don't they? It is notorious that French boys have lessons lasting about twice as long as those of English boys; what on earth are they *at* all the time? But I confess I don't really regard this as a solution. The Frenchman who has picked up a certain amount of English acquires an extraordinary glibness which makes it possible for him to pour out fresh diatribes hardly less confusing than the old; wherever his meaning becomes quite unintelligible, he helps it out by saying "N'est-ce pas?"; and it seems rude to interrupt him and say, "Non, ce n'est pas." And whereas in French, if the worst comes to the worst, you can always say "Pardon?" which is the opposite of "Parfaitement", we have no word for "Pardon?" in English, having been trained in the nursery never to say "What?" Long ago,

when it was thought that I might come to something, a misguided French-Swiss student wrote a thesis about me and my
works, heaven help him, for a doctorate. He insisted on
coming to interview with me, which was very jolly of him,
and in English. All the time he kept telling me that my
thought was very much influenced by some word which I
could not catch. It was either Royalism or Realism, but his
pronunciation made this uncertain, and it seemed brutal to ask
him which he meant. So I went on trying to answer his
questions in a non-committal way; and to this day I do not
know whether he put me down as a Royalist or a Realist. That
is the kind of thing which would create quite serious complications, if it occurred in the sphere of diplomacy.

There is another objection; the French do not, like the
English, make things easy when they are talking a foreign
language by trying to pretend that they have understood when
they haven't. They hold up the conversation by demanding
to have things explained to them; and nearly always what they
want to have explained is the inexplicable. The Abbé Bremond, in a passage of his which I was reading lately, says that
the French have no word for humbug. That would not matter
much; for indeed the word has largely disappeared from our
own vocabulary. But it would be difficult for one of his
fellow-countrymen to talk English for ten minutes to one of
our own without coming across the word "bogus". Then
the trouble begins. "Bogus? Tiens, qu'est-ce que veut dire
ce mot, bogus?" To which the Englishman's reply would be,
"Oh, bien, il veut dire que ce n'est pas vrai, vous savez, n'est
pas exactement réel . . . je crois que vous n'avez pas un mot
tout à fait comme ça" and so on. The intimacy of the cultural
relations is fatally disturbed when you come across a chap who
doesn't know what "bogus" means; I mean to say, dash it
all. The Englishman begins to watch his step, to avoid the
idiomatic and the conversational; and with that the whole

interview degenerates into a feeble series of exchanges about the weather and the prospect for the Boat Race. It's no good trying to argue with a fellow who doesn't know what you mean by "bogus".

Another solution, which would be welcomed, I suppose, by at least one in five of our fellow-countrymen, is that English people should give up trying to learn French altogether, except, of course, those who intended to go into the Foreign Office or the consular service. In that case, I suppose all future conversations between ordinary English and ordinary French people would have to be conducted in some neutral tongue; it might be Latin pronounced like French, or Esperanto pronounced like English, or German pronounced like nothing on earth. But such a compromise would involve fresh dangers in its turn, or positive misunderstanding. I prefer, therefore, as I say, to leave the prescription of remedies to others, and to content myself with this tentative diagnosis of one among the numerous causes which make the *entente cordiale* difficult to work out in every-day practice. But I daresay I may be completely out of date. It may be that the rising generation of Englishmen talks French with a fluency which leaves its Continental friends gasping for breath. It may be that I myself am a lonely psychological phenomenon, and that even my contemporaries do not share the difficulty I find in putting the stuff across. But why is it that when I come across the word *mousse*, masculine, as I did the other day, I know at once that it means a cabin-boy, having learned, fifty years ago, a list of the masculine nouns in E mute; and yet, when I emerge from the train at Paris, all my carefully prepared phrases are scattered about on the winds of the Gare du Nord, and I find myself, now as ever, reduced to the degrading formula, "Où est le Cook's homme?"